ANONYMOSITY

JOURNALS 2011 - 2012

CHRISTINE FONTANA

VirginiaDiddit

Published by VirginiaDiddit in 2025
Melbourne, Victoria, 3000
www.virginiadiddit.com

Copyright © Christine Fontana 2025
The moral right of Christine Fontana to be identified as the author of this work has been asserted.

All rights reserved. Apart from any fair dealing for the purposes of study, research, criticism, review or as otherwise permitted under the Australian Copyright Act, no part of this publication may be reproduced, stored in a retrieval system, or transmitted, in any form or by any means, electronic, mechanical, photocopying, recording or otherwise, without the prior written permission of the copyright owner/publisher.

National Library of Australia Cataloguing-in-Publication entry available for this title at www.nla.gov.au

Title: Anonymosity, by Christine Fontana
ISBN: 978-1-923221-08-6 (Paperback)
ISBN: 978-1-923221-09-3 (Ebook)

Cover design and typsettting: Christine Fontana

CONTENTS

1. Introduction ... i
2. January 2011 ... 1
3. February 2011 ... 5
4. March 2011 ... 14
5. April 2011 ... 19
6. May 2011 ... 28
7. June 2011 ... 34
8. July 2011 ... 46
9. August 2011 ... 56
10. September 2011 ... 59
11. October 2011 ... 69
12. November 2011 ... 75
13. December 2011 ... 84
14. January 2012 ... 99
15. February 2012 ... 120
16. March 2012 ... 125
17. April 2012 ... 133
18. May 2012 ... 148
19. June 2012 ... 152
20. July 2012 ... 154
21. August 2012 ... 160
22. September 2012 ... 167
23. October 2012 ... 172
24. November 2012 ... 180
25. December 2012 ... 185
26. Acknowledgements ... 199

To my children xx

Introduction

It's hardly appealing to open an introduction that begins with such joyful words as *lesser, diminished, broken*, and *subdued*, but these are the words that describe the person I found as I worked through this [fourth] volume of the *Vagina-Mite* series. It was a shock, actually, to find the same pepped up spirit, but with the volume turned down.

As the title suggests, *Anonymosity* captures a gradual and conscious retreat into hiding, despite remaining very much in the world of people. Shorter than the other volumes so far, it's not surprising that for me these years are characterised by what I haven't recorded. I'm relieved that although what I have recorded amounts to rummaging through bins to find leftover scraps of happiness, I did find them, and they're in there somewhere. Along with the usual struggle to balance art with life, surviving family and domestic chaos, and sometimes domestic bliss. Reflections on writing, goes without saying. Same old same old, and yet different.

[In]discretion

In the interests of addressing the nature of life-writing without actually addressing it [again], l repeat here that the introduction to *Vagina-Mite* – the first volume in this series – applies to all volumes, and contains:

> ...*a necessary reflection on the nature and impact of personal writing; the delicate handling of people's privacy while satisfying the compulsion to record life with candour; subjectivity as the default setting in the reader/writer relationship when it comes to memoir formats; and the outrunning of the [thievin', violatin'] AI machine. It also explains the performative nature of writing about private life on a public platform, and affectations adopted in the construction of a strong*

> alter-ego (which increase in frequency according to the degree of stress younger-me was experiencing, and which older-me has diligently cleaned up).

In summary:

Four volumes in and I'm over writing introductions, so naturally I've grown fond of my expedient little hashtag collection. If they're worth repeating once, they're worth repeating twice. This is more or less what the[se] years looked like:

> *Hashtag art and motherhood and all of the complications that go with it. Hashtag Australian writer. Hashtag domestic life, the aftermath of a marriage, the raising of an angry teenager. Hashtag the joys of motherhood, hashtag the struggle. Hashtag I'm an idiot, hashtag I am not. Hashtag art and economics, hashtag what was I thinking. Hashtag why didn't I just get a normal job. Hashtag I tried, hashtag I failed. Hashtag I succeeded, hashtag I had no idea what I was doing. Hashtag Tourette's, that simmering, bastard thing. Hashtag love, hashtag sex, hashtag too-much-information. Hashtag the end of sex as we know it. Hashtag queer relationships, hashtag hetero, hashtag unconventional family structures. Hashtag Mother wrote a book, hashtag she shouldn't have done that. Hashtag now what [?]. Hashtag how we mess up our kids. Hashtag school refusal and its poor cousins: cleaning-bedroom refusal and doing-dishes refusal. Hashtag undiagnosed neurodivergence. Hashtag perpetual student. Hashtag overcoming introversion, hashtag succumbing to introversion. Hashtag – ultimately – life.*

―――

Anonymosity
Journals 2011 – 2012

January 2011

Wednesday, 12th January, 2011.

Woe is...
I almost wrote this in the middle of the night. Was so wide awake my brain was screaming. Whatever was being killed out there was taking a long time to die.

At least owls and tawny frogmouths eat their prey. Still. Bit long.

Didn't want to sleep because I knew I'd have to wake up to today. Didn't like today before it even started.

Lost the last thread of it a few days ago. Would love more than anything to be alone for long enough to resume my project work. Not gonna happen.

So, today. This is my first brain-dump.

First-Born again, two nights ago. The argument defied logic. Son stood between us, as guardian. He no longer tries reason. Tells them outright that what they're saying is wrong.

I feel sorry for First-Born because it's two against one. But they start it. They prolong it.

I finally invited some friends over. To play taiko and be bonhomienous. It was really nice. Seems a long time ago now. After a couple of years of telling me I should invite more friends over, First-Born two nights ago told me that my friends are losers. After speaking to them for only five seconds. Maybe ten.

So anyway, I couldn't sleep, and now I'm groggy and the day looks as shit from this end as it looked from the other. [Fuck.]

But am going to get my sense of self back. Have found it hard to write this for so long. You really do start believing you don't matter. To anybody. Which of course, I know none of us do.

Hence, no writing. But the brain-dump so necessary. We don't need to matter to speak.

That's my lesson and I'll re-learn it. All of those things I want to write about but don't. No self, told you. Until now.

Tuesday, 18th January, 2011.

Failed Romantic

The good thing about my studio flooding is that it made me throw things out. I LOVE throwing things out. The less residue of me in the world the better, and gosh knows I've left a lot of that lying around.

Throughout my life I've written on anything made of paper. What, did I think every thought needed to be thunk out loud? How compulsive can a person be? Anyway, I hate that person. She needs to be binned.

On my long wall of now-wet bookcases, I found some of my old manuscripts. When I was pregnant with Son I'd put First-Born to bed and then stay up 'til a hundred o'clock every night to write. I'd also write while they slept in the afternoon. Not because I had anything to say; I still didn't know if I really had a novel in me, or that I'd ever be a fiction writer, because I was too immature to know what story really was. I thought story had to be something really imaginative, or fantastical, and worried that if I tried I'd be faking it. All I did was love words. I wasn't ready for sophisticated story yet.

So I started writing romance novels. Faking it willingly, because the one thing I did know is that I was writing constantly anyway; in my head, on paper, on cash receipts. I needed to make money and didn't know what else to do.

Imagine me being romantic! Fuck off. But anyway, there was a pot of gold at the end of the Mills & Boon rainbow, and I wanted to survive by dipping my fingers into it. So I started reading the things, and I enjoyed them. I admired the writers and their craft, and took it very seriously. Escapism = very cool.

It turns out I'm not even capable of fake-romantic. I couldn't do it. I wrote two and a half before I gave up. One of the rejections said that I was *'too downbeat'*. That's because I tried to be political in a romance novel. Which other people had done really well, but not me. I didn't even know good shoe brand names. Did I even understand the kind of romance that people wanted?

Anyway, wot fun finding the manuscripts. While stripping my studio to bits I sat down with the box and started reading. I'd kept them for sentimental reasons but have finally thrown them out; they really sucked. They were funny, and clever, but so stupid and young and wrong. Political and yet naive. One of them was set in a fat-farm, my heroin dressed up in a padded fat suit when she met the devilish man she was going to fall for. There was a clever pummelling of chests in there somewhere. She said something about reserving her help for small animals and then saying '*rodent*' under her breath. I'm noting these things for my benefit, not yours. Now that they're in the bin that's all I have left.

I feel good that there's one less box full of my brain matter in the world. How much lighter the planet feels. How positively clean[er] my life.

Wednesday, 19th January, 2011.

Would the Real PM Please Step Forward

Lately I can't help being repulsed by Julia PM. She's become wooden in her new role, and can't walk. Who makes her wear those high heels? It's debasing to be so desperately female-ish when your feet clearly need to be flat to function. (Really I'm not repulsed by her, on a physical level, but the female dress code.)

What I really can't stand are the platitudes, particularly evident in all manner of PM flood commentary. Perhaps it's the media, but all we see her doing is comforting the people with useless and repetitious conversation that's too shallow for water that deep.

I don't doubt her sincerity, but let's make an obvious comparison: look at KRudd PM. He's out there with his pants rolled up to his knees and (oh lawdy, please no) black socks in his runners, all sopping wet. His shirts are patched with sweat. He's ACTIVELY helping on the ground; lifting and grunting and really being there in a practical sense. No performance, just pure human being.

If Julia took her heels off and got her feet wet I'd respect her so much more. But the more I see, and the more she speaks, the more she's seen waddling around in those impractical shoes, the more like a mannequin she becomes every day. I wish she'd just relax and be natural. Doesn't seem human anymore. Such a pity.

February 2011

Wednesday, 2nd February, 2011.

Secret Sainthood

The ye olde's at work say a lot of nice things to me, especially now that I'm working there almost every day. They even get upset when I don't work, and ask me constantly when they're going to see me again.

But today one them upped the ante. She pulled me aside, took my protectively-gloved hand in hers, and told me that I'm *'the friendliest nurse here'*. (I'm not a nurse; I'm a Food Services Assistant. But I'll take the unofficial promotion in my stride.) She told me that she sees me working and that I smile all the time and make everybody happy. *'It costs nothing to make people happy.'*

Which is good because I'm a cheapskate.

Anyway, it made me feel both good and sad at the same time. Because I've kind of shut myself away from almost everybody, but there I am being quietly appreciated. Things like this make the thankless task less thankless. But still, it's not something that'll make it into a performance review, which just goes to show how personal interactions mean so little in this carefully documented world. On paper anything good evaporates and I just work away anonymously.

Also, I can't tell anybody what she said to me, or what they all say to me, because any personal compliment that means a lot to this unloved-feeling person would come out sounding like bragging, and might make my colleagues feel bad. And it highlights how awful loneliness can be when you're trapped, because I'm valued by people who hardly know me, therefore it's not really value. All they're loving is the surface kindness. I just like them, is all. They make me happy, too. (When they're not being selfish cnuts. You should see some of them demand their coffee before the others have even been fed – they're ruthless.)

So there's my sainthood. One colleague witnessed the conversation. Would these old people like me if they knew me better? I'd probably horrify them if I said everything I'm thinking. Maybe that's why kids and old people love me the most. And I love them. Suggests to me that I fear everybody in between. That I'm more comfortable on the periphery, where I don't doubt anything, and shit-scared of grown-up interaction.

Time to stop this hiding away business, I want proper love now. Every schmaltzy drop of it I can suck from the world.

Monday, 7th February, 2011.

Excruciation

I don't know why I thought it was such a good idea returning to an old manuscript to kill time. Or to use time more constructively, wot with summer so-far being all about paid employment and a restless home life. Just, a woman at work made some conspiracy theory comment that stunk of superstition, and it related to the subject of this particular manuscript, so the lightbulb went *ping* above my head.

I thought, *rework that old manuscript!* Even though I'd shelved it as a thing of the past. So that I'd at least have something useful to focus on.

That strategy worked, I've gotten my gumption back and have been able to concentrate. Unfortunately, though, I've discovered that I suck. And again I'm upset that it's taken me so, so long to mature (as a person, as a writer, as an artist) when other people come along and mature before they're even thirty. How did I get to be this old and still be so stupid?

The manuscript's *awful*. It earned me so much praise, and people threw the publishing word around about it. I doubted them but also held onto that praise. Now that my full vision's been restored I can see my immaturity in the writing, and am so embarrassed.

Have all of my successes so far been accidents? Am I really as bad as I think I am? I suspect so. And yet I was reading poetry last night (other people's poetry) and so much of it is also bad. I don't know how the publishers don't see it, unable to sort the wheat from the chaff. I don't know how the writers can bear to present some of their work. Why aren't they embarrassed?

Have I lost my capacity for judgement? Do I really think I have the right to judge? Am I reading through pooh-coloured glasses?

I'm making myself read to the end, and I'm making notes on the off chance that I can salvage the clever bits (there are quite a few of those, granted) so that I can redraft it into something cleaner. It'll never be an artful story. To tell the truth, I don't think I can even stand to do what I plan. I hate the sight of it. But I'll persist and see what happens.

I give it three more days. If I can stand myself for that long.

Friday, 11th February, 2011.

Excruciation – Revised

The self-loathing was spectacular, but I forced myself to keep reading and it turns out those middle bits I hated so much were just blips in an otherwise okay thing. Not okay in that I think it could be published; it's still more rubbish than not. But after my last re-write (two years ago now?) it's so much better-crafted than it was originally that I have a new respect for my ability.

I needed that. I've been beating myself over the head for being so pathetic. Am still working on the manuscript to see how much I can cut and rearrange, and it keeps looking better. Maybe they were right...? Is that possible? I might even spend money on a manuscript appraisal to find out. If I can get over the things I find problematic. Like chapter length, and overall length (too much!).

I don't know. All I know is that this summer's been horrendous, all about earning money and surviving home-life and a flooded studio. Being able to focus on the manuscript has me working hard, every day, before going off to my day job. A good remedy for wasted time. It also makes me realise that the previous years haven't been wasted. I still think I've taken longer than everybody else to mature, but I *have* matured. The evidence is there in front of me.

What I do with it now I don't know. Push the way a person needs to push to get something published? Put it back on the shelf and leave the past behind, the way I want to? Is that gutless? I can't stand the publishing game. I don't have much push left in me. We'll see. For now I'll remain secretly up-myself over the [semi] quality of the thing and keep going. Because that's better than laying down dead.

Saturday, 12th February, 2011.

What's That Got to Do with the Price of Milk?

You won't often hear me say *forget fish*, but milk needs us more right now. Coles and Safeway are the enemy, waging their price war.

It's dangerous for a society to expect food to be so cheap. There's a ripple effect. It encourages us as a people believe we deserve shit for free. It leads to an abuse of resources and ultimately waste. It distorts reality in terms of human beings understanding what it means to subsist as animals living on a material planet. It devalues the worth of a farmer's labour and a cow's life. It leads to an ultimate devaluing of our own time and – yes – lives.

You cannot remove yourself from the act of subsistence.

I wish Australians weren't kept so ignorant. Our food should NOT be this cheap. I wish they shoved Marxist theory up people's nostrils as compulsive school curriculum, so that nobody would be allowed out into the world without a good understanding of the process of value determination. So that they'd know it eventually effects how their own labour and produce is valued.

Distortion is the best word to describe the problems with Western consumerism. And if we let corporations get away with it, because *oh my isn't cheap milk wonderful*, then we're bigger motherfuckers than they are.

Friday, 18th February, 2011.

Anus-Faced

Obviously sensing the fug of existential crisis about me, one of my students gave me a *Good Weekend* clipping, a column in which John

Olsen says *'Depression... often hits artists around 40, with loss of confidence...'*. Good to know it's only my age (almost 42!!) that's making all of this work seem so pointless.

The crazy thing is that because I've been working such every-day shifts in the kitchen, the pointlessness of me is really hitting home. I want to be content with working and living, but without the rest of it (books/art, art/books; not just the things themselves, but the doing of these things) I feel so empty. And now that I'm writing again, with full knowledge of how pointless that activity really is, I feel trapped in this cycle of needing more, *despite the more I'm needing being such a stupid waste of life.*

Does that even make sense? I'm saying I *don't want* to want more. So when I did a particularly writery thing this morning (a submission which involved putting something out there a little) I felt like shit. I still feel like shit. I had to go and swim it off, and swam so slowly my brain had no choice but to also slow down. And still I resent having to go to work this afternoon, when I want so badly to stay home and... work. Work towards NOTHING.

Why do we do it? I mean, the humiliation of it all. The only cure for it right now is housework. Somebody's gotta vacuum the floor.

Sunday, 20th February, 2011.

Once More with Pictures

One of my taiko friends is also an artist-slash-book-lover – whose art I *love* but that's another story – and we go gallery-hopping after classes, which is such a nice thing (also another story), and this weekend we made our way to the State Library to see *'Look!'*, the picture book illustration exhibition.

You can imagine the hyperventilation that goes on in the place. Interesting to note, the kids (gallery was full of 'em) all stayed put in the middle section where copies of the books were splayed over the seats. I hardly saw any of them looking at the actual artwork. That's because image + story is exciting. What good is it if you can't hold it in your hands and have your mind rocked by narrative innards?

Anyway, Taiko/Tea-Party Friend not only picked favourites but numbered them from one to three, the sequence being very important to her. So odd. I just acknowledge my favourites and love them all equally, for different reasons. Some of them I already own, but I'd never heard of *Fox* (written by Margaret Wild) before. Ron Brooks' illustrations were impasto-y blocks of pure bliss. We both kept returning to his work, and on the way out I bought the book.

In my ambition to become a more decent domestic cook, after the galleries I let Tea-Party Friend drag me to the market to buy fish (I had to overcome such guilt to do this, and apologised to my dead-fish tattoo as I handed over the money) and to an Asian grocer to buy such mysterious things as mirin and kombu dashi. (The words just roll off my tongue, as though I'm cultured now?). Point being: I couldn't leave the book in the car. I had to carry it under my arm and open it every now and then for a flick through.

That's *love*.

But I didn't read it until I hopped into bed, and what an amazing story. Very simple, but it had me holding my breath quite literally in anticipation of what would happen. That anticipation was dark and fearful. An incredibly powerful little story that taps into the wellspring of human awfulness (anthropomorphised). How do kids handle that kind of dread? Or do they not expect human horribleness like I do? Luckily it's okay to hold your breath because you know it won't last long enough to kill you. I didn't expect to be quite so moved.

I wonder how many people leave that exhibition wanting to be book illustrators. For all of the things I do, I hesitate over this one. Started playing with a project a couple of years ago, and it's still very much on my mind, but I haven't committed much time to it. I haven't even resolved the story. I only have the bare bones of it and am kind of letting the feel of stylistic choices sink in and evolve. A little too slowly, and with zero confidence. And yet, when you watch the artists speak on video, it seems like such a good life. It doesn't make sense not to follow your impulses.

Isn't this what I should be doing? Perhaps one day? Perhaps even soon?

Chris Fontana

Tuesday, 22nd February, 2011.

She'll Be Apples

I just saved the lives of two apples. As much as I love that I've provided a feast for the rosellas and other birds frolicking around down in that sunshine, I looked at my apple tree and its last two surviving fruit and made my way down to the garden. I hung a net.

At the beginning of December the tree was full of baby apples, in ways that make other people use words like *laden* and *fecund*. I'll stick with full. And I cared so much about that – it's what I'd been waiting for since I planted it years ago. Before now it's given me two or three perfect fruit each season. Real apples, with *flavour*.

After Ex-Husband poisoned the garden before Xmas, even though I stood on the balcony and begged him not to poison around the fruit trees, I stopped caring about the garden, and have neglected it since. But going down there today, I felt that love again for the first time. I didn't want to leave the garden in the same way I don't want to leave the house when I'm working on a project. I hate that I have to go to work today.

Maybe there's residual poison in those apples, I don't know. What a thing it is, to struggle against sadness. It reveals to me how much other people have the power to poison the spaces I live inside, and how that affects the way I am when I'm here.

Fucken WAH, First-Born would say. They're probably right.

Wednesday, 23rd February, 2011.

The Devastatingest Dog Story

I finally found our copy of *The Digging-est Dog* (by Al Perkins – one of the Cat-in-the-Hat series' classics), which I used to read to my children *all the time*. I've been carrying it around in my bag, in case I happen to drop in on Prodigal Friend, because I keep promising to read it to her son.

Talking to her last night I again mentioned it, and was inspired to take it out of my bag to give it a quick read. I was only intending to read the first page but got addicted and couldn't put it down.

So how awful to discover that it's the Worst Bedtime Story Ever. Worst *anytime* story.

The text is clunkier than I remember but I forgave that because good enough for when I was young = good enough for my kids when they were young = good enough for any era. But when Sammy Brown said he was going to take Duke back to the store because he made an honest but dopey mistake, I was horrified. What kind of message is that giving to kids? Be good or we'll sell you into slavery? Does Sammy Brown not remember that cold stone floor?

And the almost drowning bit, well. Prodigal Friend's son would have shat himself.

I've always loved reading picture books, but I suspect I'm only now beginning [or returning] to read them as a child would. As in, I've loved the stories, but now I remember what it's like to be hit by a concept when you're young. I can imagine a child exploring the idea with pure and uninformed terror. A thing presented to them through an approved cultural artefact as concrete as a book, and delivered by adults who have authority over The Way the World Is. I can just see my kids thinking about Duke being sent back, and the inherent message: *if you're bad, you'll be abandoned.*

So now I have to ask myself what damage I might have done to my kids. First-Born especially, who has/d issues with familial security and self-worth, and who happened to spend a lot of time in the time-out corner, because they were a very intense and occasionally destructive child. (Very spunky, them. I handled the time-out situation very carefully, but was I careful enough? And wouldn't I have sometimes been at my wit's end?)

Did *The Digging-est Dog* erase my child's happiness? Did I make a mistake by allowing nostalgia to cloud my judgment? How do I undo something like that? I really hate it when political correctness is taken to extremes when it comes to childhood culture these days, as though children are delicate little flowers that need a lot of protection from normal human concerns. But when I look at something like this, and it reminds me of the disproportionate intimidation of my xtian (catholic school) upbringing, where my brain worked so hard to fathom unreasonable extremes, I'm ready to jump on that bandwagon.

Although it's not really a bandwagon, is it. It's common sense, the kind that you apply when you edit something. A belated attention to detail on my part. (*Bugger.*)

One Day in February, 2011.

Forty-One

I am.

Another Day in February, 2011.

Forty-One

I'm not anymore, and never will be again.

March 2011

Sunday, 13th March, 2011.

Restoration

I don't think it's a particularly sexy thing to have spent my summer tending to walls. All of that painting and mending. But I am kind of in love with my white walls. And it did keep me off the streets.

I allegedly went too far, though. I've been eyeing off the mural I painted on the staircase wall, which I'd started to hate. It stunk of the past, and it stunk of me, and being into self-obliteration I thought it had to go. So yesterday I finally got to it with a white primer. I erased myself. I was originally planning to paint a new mural-y kind of thing, but when I saw how clean the other white walls white looked, I realised that this house could do with less me in it.

When I started painting over it, it felt a little like sacrilege. I can't win. These are the difficult things we have to do, however, and I went to work afterwards with a clean slate behind me.

But then last night, after a particularly difficult "family discussion" that took us into the wee small hours, Son came downstairs to say goodnight and on his way back up stopped short. He let out a really disappointed *'Awww – why did you paint over that? I liked having that there'*, or something like that, and it took me by surprise. My kids never say anything about liking anything I do. What a sweet thing, to be crushed by my actions.

So of course I now feel guilty. The reality is, it was difficult to paint that mural because the surface was so slippery, and it seemed clunky to me, because I paint differently now that I work with oils.

Anyway, now I'll have to paint the new image after all. For Son. Who appears to not-think I need to be obliterated from the house. That's nice.

Chris Fontana

Monday, 21st March, 2011

Post-Impossible

The reason something's called impossible is because it's *not possible* to do it. So having undertaken two impossible things before the end of last working week was possibly a bad move on my part. One was a question of rights [mine], the other a good thing that'll never happen.

The rights one is probably causing a small ripple in offices somewhere. It involved writing a letter to my previous university, asking to resume my PhD, which was so close to resubmission it's terrible that I walked away from it. My action, but undertaken in the face of glaring hurdles that resulted from the inadvertently careless actions of other people. I can't stress that enough: they weren't being mean, they just didn't take enough care.

I feel very uncomfortable about it. It's not a thing I wanted to do. I went to visit one of my old teachers, who jumped ship and is currently Head of School elsewhere. I wanted to resume the PhD there, and was in his office to ask for advice on if and how I could do that. I felt great shame being there, and feel great shame remembering the meeting, which revealed to me how small I've become. I cried. My voice wobbly, my face collapsing, barely holding it together. Too late once I was in there to realise that I was in no state [psychologically] to be doing this Big Thing. Too obviously broken by life, and not a good bet to take on.

So, he talked me out of it, said that if I submitted the thesis there I'd have to start my candidature all over again. (Really? Why?). He advised instead that I send a letter to my old university, telling them I'd sought legal advice and that I wanted to return and complete. He said they'd take me back. Being this small, I'm not so sure.

Legal action isn't my style. In fact it's completely out of character, so I feel like shit. I was advised to detail what had gone wrong, and had to write these wrong things in such a way that they came across as nice and forgiving (which *is* true to character). But with the mention of legal advice, I suspect it doesn't matter how nice you're trying to be, you're going to be pigeon-holed as adversarial.

Maybe I should have questioned that advice. Or better yet, ignored it. Too late now. I don't want to hear the response of those discussions but know I must. And even if it's in my favour, how horrible to have to ask for somebody else's mistakes to be corrected. And how crazy not to have had the balls to ask before now, without resorting to this approach.

Such a doormat. Until I grew these hulking bureaucracy-bashing balls, albeit fake ones. I can only hope that something happens soon – I'm pretty sure these things shrink if not fed on a well-balanced diet of [fake] power.

The good thing, don't even bother. I mean it about the never-happening. Let's leave it at that.

Saturday, 26th March 2011

A Bit o' Sublime with a Lentil Soup Chaser

How many universes can you have collide in one day and still survive? After a morning saturated with Impossible Plan activities, I took myself off to see *Howl*, just by my lonesome, with more realistic plans to catch up with my favourite ever A friend afterwards. Now I'm trying to work out just how big a suck I am, because I expected to enjoy *Howl*, but I didn't expect to be so bowled over purely by the delivery of words.

For serious. When the credits started rolling my eyes were watering. I dabbed with my fingertips and realised I was crying from some antiquated state of rapture. A whole movie framed by the reading of a poem – try explaining the power behind *that* to other people. You just can't. What a beautiful man (Allen Ginsberg), and how wonderful that he lived and spoke himself out loud like that.

Sigh, sigh and *sigh*. I wasn't too enamoured by the animation. I think that element of the movie will date too quickly? A combination of good ideas and partially simplistic design. Maybe that's just me becoming an art snob.

Anyway, this was the state I was in when I caught up with the lovely Friend A in a café in Carlton, over pumpkin and lentil soup. Can a day get any more perfect?

Yes! It can. Many heightened states later, I was walking down Flinders Street when I saw my art theory teacher. (What are the chances! In the middle of a crowded city!) When I said *hello* she asked me where I'd been, I mentioned *Howl* with residual rapture leaking from my voice, so she said *let's do a cup of tea,* and I was transported to Universe Four for the day.

Long and animated discussion about all sorts of everythings. I texted Young Studio Friend afterwards = she thinks I'm a teacher-whore because the teachers all seem to like me. She's wrong, not all of them do. And actually that scares the crap outa me because after I talk to them I always think I've said the wrong thing or am too obviously young and naive. (Did I just call myself young? Relatively, let's say.)

But anyway, onto the train and then back home and there, being delivered into my in-box was the portal to Universe Five, a notification that Impossible Plan #1 is going to happen.

All of that and I still had time to cook me children a roast dinner before going for a long walk last night.

If I count my current projects they're not all going to fit onto ten fingers. May have to count also on my toes. Am making up for that sad summer of almost no doings whatsoever. I don't know whether to be excited or overwhelmed. Strangely, I think I can do it all. Even the saving-the-world part. Did I not mention that? Another day, maybe. If I even have time.

Sunday, 27th March, 2011.

I Want I Must Have

They say a change is as good as a holiday, but they're wrong. I know this because I actually had a holiday last weekend, and then when I was back at work during the week there were changes afoot, and they were nowhere near as good as that holiday. That's empirical evidence.

About this holiday; I want it to be my real life. We (my family) went to our little town in East Gippsland, on the high plains, where Mum spent the first eight years of her life. We visited the place on the riverbend where the murderer's hut she lived in still stands, although it's starting to collapse a little. We walked to the gold mines where my grandfather worked every day. We had picnics and then went back into town to feast and drink wine.

We're all in love with this place, and wish we'd re-discovered it earlier. I want to buy property there, and therefore need suddenly to be rich enough to live in two places. One house there, as ramshackle as it needs to be, I don't mind. And one here.

A bolt-hole to escape to, somewhere all of my people can visit and camp and escape to also. Because imagine being able to disappear into deep quiet and forest with your writing projects and your art projects whenever you need to. Away from all of this stinking noise.

So anyway, there was this house on upwards of 50 acres, and I could probably afford it [HAH] if it weren't a gazillion kilometres away, only it was sold within days of my establishing a neat little daydream over its undulating expanse. And now I'm bereft. What am I going to spend my imaginary money on? Must I always stay grounded in the real world? *Fuck*.

April 2011

Friday, 8th April, 2011.

All Talk, No Action
That's why I'm wagging school today. I've put so much energy into research and organisational stuff that I haven't had any think time, let alone dabble-in-ink time. (Rhyme unintentional.) Feeling empty because of it, like an unfinished person. So today is for arting. Except, it's *sunny*. Maybe the last sunny day for a while, and that's a washing day if ever I've seen one. Just one more load, I swear, and when that's hung out on my balcony I'll be down here with ink and paper.

I might have to turn the computer off first.

I finished with a hard-core theoretical presentation on Wednesday, and suddenly here's the world again. I thought I'd imagined it. So yesterday, also a good washing day, also spent at home = met up with Mum for a walk along the reservoir wall. The drought island that's been sitting in the middle of that sinking mass has been submerged completely, by actual water. We've watched it since it first appeared as a thirsty little peak, at which we shook our heads and lamented the precariousness of this city and its resources. Yea, we're all saved.

Tuesday, 12th April, 2011.

There's an Up Side to Everything
The good thing about having an art crisis is that it's distracting me from the writing crisis I should probably be having right now.

Thursday, 14th April, 2011.

Not Laughing. Much.

It's politically incorrect to laugh at a disabled person, so I'm starting with a disclaimer. That is, I'm not laughing at him, I'm laughing at the situation.

I could tell over the phone that the insurance man was older. One of those gruff voices that only half articulates, as though he's speaking more to himself than to you, and you just happen to be overhearing. A guesswork thing, as in, did he say such and such? I think he said such and such, therefore I'll prepare for such and such and hope I've gotten it right.

So he ended up at the wrong house, not surprised. Then I called and he called and he somehow ended up at the right house, and I watched him pull his car in at the top of my *very steep* driveway.

The first thing that got out of his car was a pair of crutches. Followed by an old-ish man with one leg. Old man with one leg plus crutches at the top of my driveway equals *oh fuck*. I stared and thought *you've got to be kidding me*. I didn't laugh yet because I was puzzled about what to do. Should I... what? What really? No way I could let him bring his car down, because from memory other people don't seem to manage to get their cars back up again. We looked at each other, we negotiated the car situation, he decided to go down on foot and crutch. It's all paved, but still. I was relieved I'd trimmed and re-mulched the garden that morning, because he started off on the stones but then went to the steps. I felt so guilty for not living on flat land. I was sure he was gonna go arse over.

So, what's the etiquette for this one? Do you help a disabled man by holding onto his elbow if you don't really know him? Are you supposed to ignore the disability in the face of potential fall-down-driveway death, just to allow for dignity? I did neither of those things. I did all of the draw-attention-to-it things, and that's when I had to stop myself from laughing. Especially when he got inside and asked where the problem is and I had to say *'Downstairs'*. Kinda cruel, to make him assess properties in this area. (If only I'd thought of driving my car up to get him. That woulda been smart.)

Anyway he was lovely, and he didn't die. And his son-in-law is the brother of the man who had this house built and lived in it with wife and family for twelve years, before building next door and living there for one, who happens to be my ex-husband's boss. He did his assessment and my studio will get new carpets and bookcases. The house-front boards will be fixed and all will be well. And it was much easier for him to get back up than it was to get down.

As he drove off I shook my head at my unpreparedness for such a situation, and wondered if I should install a slide beside my driveway. Which of course I won't. But in future maybe I should consider asking people I haven't met how many legs they have before I give them directions to my house.

Saturday, 16th April, 2011.

Good. Very Good.

Yesterday morning I stumbled out of bed and made my way upstairs, where First-Born was cooking in the kitchen. They'd been up all night, and I've been really worried about them because their nocturnalness is sometimes so pronounced. I was considering saying something about it, but hesitated because I didn't want to upset them by sounding potentially critical.

So I stood there looking at them, wondering what to do, not wanting to do nothing but not wanting a scene, and they looked at me and I waited for them to say *Fuck off*, but they didn't. They laughed and said *'You should see the look on your face!'* and then asked me if I'd like some scrambled eggs.

I was particularly not-hungry, but I said *'Yes please'*, and then potted about while First-Born cooked. When I came back upstairs they'd placed the plates of egg and toast next to each other on the kitchen table. That's an *invitation*. So I sat with them to have breakfast. Outside was really pretty and I was facing the view. First-Born started talking about the evils of social network thingies and we kept talking for about an hour.

That's an hour of practically being normal. It was really nice. And a big relief – because without these interludes I have no idea how they're doing. After that I think they're still a bit lost, but they're doing fine, just fine.

Saturday, 16th April, 2011.

Why Would You

I bought my first beer last night. I always wonder why people train themselves to like the stuff, considering that it takes so much effort. But I was curious, so when we went out for happy-hour drinks after studio and everybody was drinking beer, and it was half the price of the house wine, and now that I like real wine I couldn't stand the idea of crappy house stuff, I thought *Okay, here goes nothing*.

Well fuck off. I had my beer and we shared chips and I passively smoked (also yuk), and I didn't feel any cooler than I had *before* I'd bought my first beer. I made it through the top centimetre, but after that it was hard going. In the end I said *'Here, have some'* to an open crowd and within seconds it was gone.

I'll never do that again. Even more awful, though, was my post-beer friend-date with Young Studio Friend. We went out for dinner, and then went to an advance screening of *Incendies*. All was well. In fact I was loving it; the performances are amazing, the cinematography likewise. But then the end happened and I was really shocked. It takes a lot to shock me, I gotta say, but my jaw dropped. It wasn't the nature of the twist in the storyline that got me, it was the stupidness of it. Something possible but unlikely, a something that transformed the quest the twins were on into a cruel kind of personal game.

If you were writing such a perfectly gripping story, why would you ruin it with such a dorky shock-value climax? Unless it's based on reality – and I don't think it is – it's just dumb.

It might be I think this because I hate neo-freudianism and this plot stunk of the stuff. But also, it belittled the personalised horror of the violent context, which is what made the rest of the story so powerful. Who in their right mind would say that plot out loud and believe it's a good idea?

We both left the cinema feeling fucked in the head. In a really dark way. I had nothing to say for the rest of the night. I'll still recommend it to people, but with a warning about the potential for disappointment, and about its spectacular narrative collapse.

Sunday, 17th April, 2011.

The Great Ongoing Mindwash

Yesterday afternoon I was at a party hosted by Prodigal Friend's two year-old son, who had a great idea for celebrating and so she ran with it (a MILK PARTY!). I didn't know until I was there that a lump of xtians would make up the bulk of the guests. It was me, our poofter friend, and them. Us and Them, if you like. (Gosh knows I like.)

It's not that I didn't know I had prejudices, but I kinda had them reinforced. Despite the fact that they were nice people. It's just, once you know they're xtians and you see them wear their faith in their personalities, coupled with the fact that you've been warned to keep your lewd sense of humour and poofter friend's homosexuality tucked in out of sight... well. That makes for a prejudice party.

The most alarming thing happened after Poofter had left. We were all in the loungeroom playing party games, when Prodigal Friend made an excited announcement to the xtians, about Her Son asking to say a prayer the day before. It was then I discovered that the xtians are from a playgroup she attends. She prompted Her Son to say it out loud, and I sat there quite stunned when he sang out *'Dear god thank you for food and friends'*. When the xtians all cheered, and Grandmother Xtian called out *'Good boy [Her-Son]!'* in a blatant show of indoctrination-in-action, I was disgusted.

That, you see, is why xtians are effing.

The strange thing is that Prodigal Friend didn't look at me. I was expecting an apologetic look, for exposing me to that filth. Or some sort of acknowledgement that she appreciated my not swearing out loud. But she gave no indication of there being something revolting happening to her son. So I had to watch these people like they were zoo animals. Partake in conversations where I learnt about them being not just effing xtians, but soy-drinking effing xtians, with kind new-age hearts. I was raised Catholic, so I mostly felt sorry for their kids, and kept observing them, trying to imagine their [soiled] world view.

I wanted to text Poofter and suggest we do an emergency intervention, but discovered that I've lost his phone number. So I went outside to play totem tennis with Prodigal's Son.

I suppose they were nice, but really how can you tell, when people are programmed to behave a certain way and you can't really see what they are? All I see are the performances of goodness. I sat there the whole time thinking about how I can't relate to xtians, and being mildly peed off that they wouldn't eat my exceptionally nice cake, because it had chocolate icing and they'd all given chocolate up for Lent.

I was also alarmed because they said that Prodigal's Son's biscuits were lovely, and Prodigal kept telling them they were my recipe. I wanted to scream because they'd cooked them all wrong, so no they weren't nice at all (how does anybody turn a moist, sweet biscuit into a dry, savoury biscuit?), which just proves how xtians are too falsely kind to their fellow human beings to even be honest about their cooking.

(This is beside the point, but HOW IS IT THAT PEOPLE THESE DAYS ARE GETTING EXCITED ABOUT BAD BISCUITS?)

Now I have a dilemma. Prodigal texted me later to tell me they all thought I was really lovely, and then she rang to tell me that Grandmother Xtian had said *'She's a lovely soul'* as soon as I'd left. The dilemma is: to accept this compliment and store it in the folder in my brain where I keep declarations of my aceness made by other people, do I have to recant my very unkind effing-xtian-critical thoughts? Or should my alleged aceness not interfere with my honest intolerance of all things xtian? And does this mean that I was being false because I wasn't really lovely on the inside, therefore the compliments are negated anyway? I don't think I was being false; I was just *being*, and most of me was *being* genuinely. I just wasn't showing my disgust at the things that disgusted me.

So yah, I'm keeping the compliment. It's mine-all-mine.

Saturday, 23rd April, 2011.

Plan B

I don't know where Son got his disgusting sense of decency and respect for others, but he certainly didn't get it from me. I've been trying to get him to help me smash the bin box that sits above our house. He insists that because it belongs to the neighbours, smashing it would be wrong. Even though it's ugly! Even though it's gotten out of control!

Bugger respect. The good thing is that he said he doesn't care if *I* smash it, which means I can at least drag him down to accomplice level, even if I can't turn him into a full petty criminal.

Not that I think it's petty. The bin box is a louvered timber cupboard that the neighbours sat above our house (their driveway opens out above us) to put their bins in, so that all they have to do is pull them out on bin day.

Fine in theory, ugly in practise. The box makes the pretty bend in our street look like somebody's old garage. Dumpy, really. Only it gets worse. They're nice people, but they ain't got no aesthetic sense. They actually stopped using the fugly box; they now don't bother putting the bins back in, so we have their ugly cupboard *and* their bins sitting above our house.

And that's not all; they fill their bin to literal overflowing, with the overflow flowething around our driveway and into our garden. There's litter everywhere.

So it's hard rubbish time, and they've pinned their bins in with their not-carefully placed hard rubbish. To solve the problem I've dragged that box forward. Under cover of darkness I tried to pull one door off and all of the slats fell loose – loudly – so I ran down my driveway to hide. I've effectively broken the thing. Now I need to drag it onto the road in the hope that it falls more to pieces, because if they don't break it up the hard rubbish won't take it. It's too big.

That's the bit Son won't help me with.

What to do? Son suggested I *ask them* to get rid of it. Crazy kid – I didn't teach him honesty, either, so I don't know how he comes up with these hair-brained ideas. Obviously I can't be honest with them, because if that doesn't work then I'll be stuck with the problem, because my vandalism will be traceable back to me. Plus I don't want to embarrass them. No, sneaking is the way to go.

Me, my combat boots and a crow bar. Sounds like a wild Saturday night for me this week. Beats reading a book.

Tuesday, 26th April, 2011.

Eggs a` la Moccasin

I don't know how somebody like me ended up being a food snob, but I think I am. It's not about poshery or anything. I'm not posh and I don't want to be. But when I eat eggs at a café I want them to be wholesome goodness *and* something better than I can make myself, or at the very least something I can make myself but never get around to.

So when Ye Olde Sister says she's taking me out for breakfast for my [belated] birthday, and arrives at my house to pick me up with Me Lovely Mother and Me Dear Old Dad in tow as a surprise, I'm as happy as all heck until she asks *'Where to?'*, and Dear Old Dad says he knows a place in the food court of the local shopping centre that *serves good omelette*. They all say *'Okay let's go there!'*. I don't stop being happy but I do start being alarmed.

A food court? Seriously? I have to work to stop the horror from overwhelming me. I've always thought it tragic that my family are okay with doing our family functions at chain restaurants or bistros attached to pokies venues et cetera, because the places are usually so noisy you can't talk and the food's expensive and *okay* but only *ordinary*-okay. The reason I think it's tragic is because I know there are smaller places that are much better, like Vietnamese restaurants and Thai restaurants and so on and so on, where the social aspect of the meal is much more special.

But anyway, back to the food court because that's where we ended up. And it was a really good breakfast company-wise. I love my family and it wasn't too loud so we talked and talked. I sat facing a window that opened up onto a corridor that housed a Dollar King variety thing shop. Dad sat in front of a magazine rack full of *Women's Weeklies*. The menu offered chips with your omelette (oh fuck off). Dad actually ordered chips with his omelette [!!].

The middle-aged man who served our food arrived at our table wearing grey tracksuit pants and a hooded sweat jacket. I could taste the saucepan and not the egg. Ye Olde Sister said *that-was-lovely* when the plates were collected. I wished I was bulimic so I could throw it up.

(Just quietly, Mum didn't like her one scungey piece of toast, which had cost her $3.20. We colluded on the side.)

But that's okay! Because it was a nice morning out. And when I think about how Mum and Dad both grew up in rustic environments where people weren't rich and food wasn't as plentiful, I realise nothing would seem wrong to them about the abundance offered by large shopping centres and their food courts. The ambience I'm wanting is nothing compared to the security the contemporary shopping centre environment represents. I should stop wanting to get away from these things, which symbolise our nation's affluence and good fortune.

Bad, ungrateful Me.

May 2011

Wednesday, 4th May, 2011.

The House Came Down

It's hard to ignore the parallel between Americans rejoicing in the streets and the munchkins dancing around singing *'Ding dong the witch is dead'*. Both tantamount to a kind of baying for blood.

When I heard the news of He Who Shall Not Be Named (OBL) being killed, I felt first sombre with respect as I would for anybody's death, and then concerned about the context in which it happened. Was it an Execution? It's starting to look that way. People are rightfully disturbed by this, even though the alternative (capture) may have caused a string of repercussive dangers.

I think it wrong for American officials to have released images of the bloodied bedroom; a violation of an intimate space on the one hand, and a politically incendiary sight on the other. I think it wrong that Hillary had the decency to look shocked during the watching of the thing as it happened, but then made declarations about America's might in such a *don't-fuck-with-the-all-powerful* way.

America needs to learn humility. Do they not get it? This is about ideology – it's not a game where there are winners. Thank goodness they performed respectful burial procedures. The whole thing is just plain ugly.

Tuesday, 10th May, 2011.

How to Un-Grow Up

Buy a scooter! Not the moped motorised type, but the manual push-with-foot type. Not the small trendy death-trap push-with-foot type other people are riding these days, but the larger non-trendy push-with-foot type.

I haven't done this amazing thing yet, but I think I will. I've wanted one since I was little and the richer friends in our street let me ride theirs. And now I've found them (Kickbikes!), in Australia, and they look like penny farthings, only daggy-er. When I told First-Born about it they said I'd have to wear a monocle and a suit to ride it, but I think I'll be okay if I just ride it in the dark. Possibly in disguise.

The only problem with this scenario is that I'm quite poor, and have agonised over the last couple of weeks about quitting my job, being upset by said job and wanting to stick it to the man. I've plotted and planned for survival on very little money, and followed the romantic notion of starving-artist as far as it'll take me, salivating over the TIME I'd have available to spend making actual ART and actual WRITING [if I quit], instead of all of this pathetic daydreaming that keeps getting interrupted by LIFE.

Fuck life. I've been very unhappy, and if this makes me happy then so be it. It could be that my craving to spend so much energy riding a scooter – flying, I tell you – and to feel my muscles stretch and push may be unrealistic now that I'm on my way to being a ye olde. Misled by memories of childhood energy, maybe?

But this daydream has at least enabled reconciling myself with continuing to work at the nursing home, despite the evil changes they've made to our working conditions. Because I can't help but acknowledge that the money I earn allows me to buy books and art materials, and outrageously expensive scooters. Plus feed my children.

I remind myself of this every time I buy a book. Every time I drive, even, because I haven't had to scrape pennies together to buy petrol. We've been living comfortably. (My version of comfortable isn't lavish, let it be said. I'm still poor, just not destitute. Yet.)

Ah bugger. All of this money talk is undoing the un-growing up that the idea of riding a scooter has achieved. I have to make a Deal with Self: if I don't still hate my job by the end of today's shift, I'll buy the scooter. Then I can ride it to work and spend my shifts looking forward to riding it home.

Something to look forward to! Perfect.

Friday, 13th May, 2011.

Have a Nice Day Or Else

I've noticed lately that the Safeway people have been aggressively friendly. Even if you gracefully ignore them by nodding and giving them cursory answers, they keep talking at you. That's when you realise they've been instructed to be-friendly-goddammit by the store managers. Probably a new policy.

Even though I've complained about the self-service checkouts and flatly refuse to use them because I want to be served by humans, I don't actually want those humans to talk at me. Except for the nice one who reminds me of Friend Alice. Apart from her, I want to be ignored in turn by checkout operators. Because shopping is like driving; I do it on autopilot and spend most of that time either trying to remember lists or daydreaming, both occupations that involve being in some kind of trance. I resent having my trance broken by false interest.

Harsh, you think? Well no – I'm pretty sure the teenage boy who asked me twice if my day had been busy tonight didn't really give a shit about my day. My own children don't give a shit about my day, and I therefore find the boy's conversational pushiness offensive. Did he realise he'd asked me twice, or was it a sign of panic at his thwarted attempts to make me feel a special bond forming between us?

The really bad thing is that it makes simple interaction inauthentic, and destroys any opportunity for real and spontaneous conversation. Which wouldn't have happened anyway because I'd just spent my spontaneous conversation reserves on my lovely neighbour from over the road, who'd tapped me on the shoulder in the fridge aisle and suggested we do drinks again soon. For the checkout boy I had nothing left. Deal, teenager. Middle-aged people don't want to talk to you, and probably won't until you're over forty.

What?! I'm so damn friendly anyway – can't I be mean sometimes? I should at least have the option of being mean. Everybody else does it, gimme a break. Niceness is good and sometimes momentary niceness can save a person's day, but you can be nice without being fake. That's all I'm saying.

Thursday, 19th May, 2011.

Less is More, Politicals.
Could media coverage of politics in this country get any more stupid? I just tried to watch George Negus's show for the third time, and I have this to say about the first two attempts at watching: I didn't learn anything new about the topics that were already familiar to me, and the topics that were new were covered so superficially that I might as well have not seen them. In fact, they were as light as bus stop conversation. Lighter.

So just now, watching him interview Julia PM, I shouldn't have been shocked by the fluff. To wind up by challenging her with a summarised opinion-of-the-masses (that the government can't govern, and that the opposition do nothing but oppose) is too much like saying '*Ha! Speak your way out of that!*'.

I mean, what's she supposed to say to that? George, you're inviting the mouthful of repetition she offered you, and you're subjecting us to it. We are, respectfully, *bored*.

Saturday, 21st May, 2011.

They Dun Left Me. Again.
First-Born is a joy to have around, and that's why it's wonderful that they've gone. They left home a week ago, saying some things that left me devastated before they left. But then when they were here to pick up a parcel last night, they had a friend with them, and they were the child I love.

First-Born makes me *laugh*. They don't joke or laugh with me anymore, but when they're around other people they're hilarious.

So anyway I, of course, have been grieving. My personality is cloaked in black mourning clothes and dark veils. But they asked me if I'd watched *Offspring,* which we'd watched together when they were here. I didn't think they gave a damn about whether I'd watched it or not, but I nodded a quick '*Yes*' and was preparing to leave the room in case they got mean again, when they asked '*Thoughts?*'.

This is confusing, because last week they said they were leaving because they can't stand me. (Which also confused me, because I thought we'd been getting along.) Now they value my opinion? For serious? Right when I was preparing to be rejected in totality.

First-Born said something or other, and [without sulking] I reminded them *'You can't stand me, remember?'*. They insisted that they'd taken those words back after they'd said them.

They didn't take them back, and saying that they *had* taken them back now is a bit like getting away with still not taking them back, because they haven't actually given an apology. A bit like when I said to Son *'You didn't wish me a Happy Mother's Day'*, and he said *'Yes I did'*, when actually he didn't, so instead of saying it again and making sure I heard it this time, claiming to have said it is a way of not having to actually say it, and getting away with it because I might be stupid enough to believe that he did.

(By the way, my kids didn't wish me a Happy Mother's Day. And before that, a Happy Birthday. My invisibility is astounding this year. Crank up the violins.)

Maybe my kids mean what they don't say. And if they don't, I'm happy to be fooled anyway. I love 'em, that's all. So First-Born's gone, and I have to let them go, hoping that they're safe and happy, and that they'll gradually gravitate back towards me.

One day, maybe, I'll recover and become the more grown-up version of who I was before I started to die inside, before I started to disappear. One week and I can feel it coming back already – optimism, for the first time probably since the last time they left.

Speaking of which, tonight smells like summer. Like happier summers from the past. Suddenly things like love and writing and art are possible. Quiet nights, and reading. It's not because First-Born's gone – that's all-over sad. It's because they're picking themselves up and doing things in the world, so I don't have to worry about them too much.

I've submitted grant applications, I've started painting again. And other things. Reading reading reading. And ahead of me, a future full of that kind of peace. Quiet, soft light. More reading. Eventually I'll people that quiet, but for now I'm happy to be alone, riding my scooter across the long reservoir wall almost every night until my legs ache. The smell of water in the cold wind. 360 degrees of sky around me. I have no idea what happens next.

———

Wednesday, 25th May, 2011.

Poison

That feeling I get, on and off, when I enter the studios sometimes. That my presence is soiling a pure environment, the young people so fresh and optimistic and unburdened. And here's me bringing in so much emotional baggage I can hardly walk under the weight of it. On those days it takes a while to warm up and shuck the darkness.

I get the same feeling when I go home to visit Mum and Dad now. Have for a long time, knowing that they know what's happening, that they know I'm faking [badly] my former cheerfulness.

So I don't visit even when I want to. When I leave the studios I often drive home the long way, up Dandenong and Ferntree Gully Road[s], which takes me right past their estate. I agonise over thinking of things I can tell them, interesting or positive or both, just so that I have an excuse to visit. I want more than anything to visit, but more often than not my tank is empty. I can't imagine even pretending to be interesting, and know that if I drop in we'll stand in the kitchen (where we all talk when we visit) and have nothing good to offer them.

Inevitably this leads me to believe that I'm entirely un-good, that to have me stand in their kitchen so empty of life would be excruciating for them. So I wave and tear up as I drive past the turnoff, hoping I'll have thought of something by the next time I go past. And I drive the rest of the way home feeling empty, and missing them so badly.

Failing them kills me just that little bit more.

———

June 2011

Wednesday, 1st June, 2011.

I Didn't Expect...

...to see First-Born on their birthday. One of the things they said to Son the night before they left was that they were going to change their name so they could cut themself off from the whole family. The way they were talking then I thought I might never see them again.

Even though I didn't expect to see them, the night before their birthday I made chocolate fudge (which is really ganache) and sent them a text saying *'I made your breakfast: Shall I drop it somewhere for you?'*. They sent back *'I don't want it.. :('*.

Then I was worried because they sounded unhappy. The sad-face emoji was the give away. But the next day they sent another text saying *'I suppose I could come over and partake in some fudge soon...'*. [!!!]

So for the second year in a row, when I expected not to see my child on their birthday, they arrived at the doorstep and I fed them fudge. And they stayed. They stayed for over an hour and talked and talked and talked. About their training, and about what they want to do, all of the things they'd refused to tell me about before.

They still won't tell me where they're living (I have actually worked it out), but we got to talking about how we're similar in very particular ways, something they would have been furious at me for in the past because they wanted to be anything but the same as me.

And so First-Born returns to me, inch by excruciating centimetre. I'm holding my breath in the hope that our life will be okay.

Friday, 3rd June, 2011.

The Singing Fruiterer

That's how I want to fall in love. I was on my way home from swimming, my face still red from the sauna, my body relaxed, my hair a curly mess from not having been brushed and not at all dry. I was buying grapes and as I approached the register at my favourite fruit shop I could hear the fruiterer singing. He's tall and dark, European of some sort, and scruffy with facial growth. His voice was deep and calm and beautiful because of the contentment. Something operatic, which I don't care for much, but the fact of singing: nice.

He asked me if I'd been at the gym and I had to shake myself out of my own head to answer. He made some joke about being dragged back out to deep water by animal conservationists last time he went swimming, and I laughed even though it took me a long minute to work out that he was calling himself a beached whale. I didn't want to leave him because I wanted to hear him sing again.

So here I am thinking about falling in love again, something I haven't thought possible for a long, long time. This is what equilibrium does to you. I'm not going to fall in love with the fruiterer, but I'm going to fall in love with somebody who sings while they work. I sing while I work, and I know what it means about feeling peaceful and content.

I wonder if the fruiterer reads books.

Saturday, 4th June, 2011.

Social Overload

It's not just that I'm a miserable old fuck. There's something else that's stopping me from socialising as much as I might usually. I have actually been socialising a bit, just enough to keep the pulse of friendships going. Mostly, though, I've shut myself away.

I was in at the studios recently, where I'll be full-time again next semester. (I went part-time for a while, was needed at home). And it occurred to me that the studios are like a living, breathing F@ceb**k. A chaos of people, all connected everywhere, in each others' space every minute of every day, and no slowing down, so little just "being". I find it strange and overwhelming. Who can keep up that social pace? Where's the introspection? How do I make being there part of a routine that I can manage? How do I connect with people properly? Do I just drift in and out?

I know it'll be different when I'm there. But still. So many friends, and really I only ever spend good and focussed time with a few of them. It reminds me of the social nature of Ex-Girlfriend-Not-Girlfriend – so much stimulus, but not enough depth (no offence, E-G-N-G).

I was talking to a friend about something really serious and he was distracted by other people also trying to get his attention. I regretted talking to him, witnessing the pull of everything, the sheer inability to stay in one headspace at any given time. And I was repulsed by how easy it is to be shallow, to touch people in such shallow ways, and then there was this fear of never finding slowness.

Maybe it's just because I'm a hundred years older than everyone and so time means something different to me. I'll have to prepare for returning really carefully. It'll be nice to be with them all again, but I don't want that many friends. Not if it's not real. (Okay so maybe it *is* because I'm a miserable old fuck. Once I'm there I'll love everybody, that's just the way it is. And it'll be wonderful.)

———

Monday, 6th June, 2011.

Home Sweet Home

Another text, telling me First-Born wants to come home. I answer cautiously. To me it's not a question, just something that has to be managed carefully. To avoid the past repeating itself. But the texts keep coming and First-Born says they appreciate the peace and the routine of home (my peace, my routine, things they hated me for). They say they want to save money. They don't feel comfortable anywhere else.

They ask permission to come home. They promise me it'll be different. I'm impressed that they asked permission, but also sad that they thought they had to.

Son wasn't pleased when I told him. He said '*They're everywhere*', meaning they take up all of the emotional space in the house, until you can't escape them. And he's right, you can't. The mess of hostility. This made me felt sorry for First-Born and also for him, because like me he's experienced this for seven years, and those are seven years none of us can undo. But they're different this time, I can feel it. They used the word "appreciate". [!!!!]

So I snuck them out of their current digs in the middle of the night. I don't think they told them they're leaving. And now they're home. I've prepared the room for them, spent more than a day moving furniture out so that they'll have more space this time. I cleaned, I made the bed, I made it all nice.

My children are both safe under my roof, and that's such a relief. I'm scared that First-Born wasn't gone for long enough, that none of us have recovered enough from the last time to cope with this time. My spirit so broken. So much crying.

But they're home. And they're friendly. And they're going to be different this time. They promised.

One Small Thought Allowed, I Guess…

The problem with not thinking is that you forget all about your ambitions for blue and end up with a nice but not-blue-enough grey. Which throws your commitment to *'doing things without over-thinking from now on so that you don't worry so much'* right out the window.

Except, it's different this time. I'm painting again: check. But instead of having to re-learn to paint all over again, the way I do if I take so much as a few weeks off, I seem to know what I'm doing. Apart for forgetting the blue, I mean. I'm not so much re-learning as I am resuming where I left off. A WHOLE YEAR AGO.

This is very *far out Brussels sprout* for an over-thinker like myself. Does this mean I'm so numb that I can't even feel fear of what I'm doing? Do I have so much warming up to do that the fear I have to overcome hasn't even happened yet? Just how dead am I, exactly?

Don't care, I guess. Feels good to be working again, and apparently not-thinking is good for me.

Memorial Fraud

My Lovely Mother's about to commit this. Because we were all there at that last holiday to her old home on the High Plains, except for Feral Brother, who lives in Tasmania. That's two parents, and eight-out-of-nine offspring. We have the photo to prove it.

Mum's enlarged one of the group photos, and wants to get the absent Feral Brother doctored in. I objected more loudly than I probably should have, and may have offended her, crushing her dreams of having One Big Happy Family hung up on her wall. But why would you do that? It's so fake. Is any one of us ever going to look at that photo and not think *Yeah but he wasn't really there*? We'll always know.

Since when did illusion become something you want fucking with your family memories?

Monday, 13th June, 2011.

A Perfect Shade of Adequate

I'm one or two steps away from finishing that painting. I can't get over how different it's been; I just go about my business, doing what I need to do, loving colour but without fear or panic. It's okay but not beautiful, and I don't need it to be beautiful, just okay is fine with me.

Does that sound even the remotest bit right? Not to me it doesn't. Since when did I become so relaxed?

And does this mean I'm officially over caring because caring is for idiots who think what they do matters? Or is it very zen, something to do with knowing that everything just is what it is? And that when my relationship with paint evolves into its latest incarnation, it will happen by doing, so doing is enough.

Where's the self-punishment? The self-deprecation? Surely I should be embarrassed to be allowed to breathe? What's wrong with me that everything feels just right?

Sunday, 19th June, 2011.

deybooting

On Friday I discovered what happens when bogans get glamorous. My niece's deb ball happened, and I was asked to take photos of many flouncy teenagers down by the local "lake". Which I did. And I tried so hard not to be political on the inside when I was smiling on the out, but there ya go – while everybody else was *oohing* and *ahhing* all I could think about was how debs are an enormous event so empty of meaning that I couldn't see the point. I had to remind myself that the point is fun (remember that? what?), and tried not to choke when somebody called out *'The stretch Hummer's here!'*.

If the word "vulgarity" slipped into my mind I'm sure I didn't mean it. It's not that I'm a naysayer, but I thought I might have to tank myself up on a few glasses of wine to see The Great Event in a more positive light. Although I was sure I'd enjoy it when I was there. Hedonism or bust.

Anyway I did enjoy it. She was so happy I couldn't help loving that she was loving it. And yes I was tanked up, the woman at the bar being very generous with the sweet wine when it came to reaching the brim of a very big glass. But that's beside the point. Who cares if the pomp is extravagant, I need to lighten the fuck up. Fun! With people I love! All of this life in me, and not nearly enough living going on. I need to be more like everybody else.

(Amendment: maybe they're not bogans. Maybe they're hipsters. Or valley girls? What *are* outer-suburban teenagers these days?)

So That's How It's Gonna Be

When First-Born came back home one of the differences that asserted itself before the samenesses took hold = they walked with me. My walk, that I've been doing every day with only subtle variations for the past twelve years. A good, demanding hill-climbing constitutional, one that makes me feel peaceful and which I'd die without.

At first there was conversation; friendly, then tolerant, then reluctant, and then it may have been conversation that involved swearing at me (f-words, c-words), but it was conversation nonetheless.

Tonight, I got home from work and was wondering if I should ask First-Born for a walk, trying to work out if they were in their swearing mood, when they finally emerged from their room wearing walking clothes and left the house. To go for a walk. Without even inviting me. To go for *MY* walk. I'm trying to see that as okay, but actually it's slap in the face.

Things are, unfortunately, what they are, which is pretty much also what they were.

So now what? How not to curl up and die? A very social weekend = teaches me that I'm happiest when I'm not here, but I also need to be here. How do I sever myself?

First plan, I think, might be to put everything in boxes as though we're moving out. So that it doesn't feel like a failed family home, but is more reflective of the long-term transition that it is. Waiting for a better life.

It'd at least be easier to keep clean, if not happy. I'd settle for that right now. Clean and simple. Something I don't want to leave when I wake up each day.

Monday, 20th June, 2011.

Scooters R Cool

Don't let anybody tell you any different. I really do fly over that wall above that body of water. And people stare. And I talk to strangers. I fly and I fly and I fly. And I talk to more strangers. And this one man, who had such a friendly face. I can do this. He was with his grandmother, walking the way I walk with my mum. He took his hood off to say hello.

I should have spoken more. I should have offered him a turn.

I can do this. The simple act of being human again, and in the world. Talking to people, and laughing with them. About my scooter.

And anyway the freedom. The smell of the air coming off the water. The cold wind. Remembering how good it feels to be in your body in the cold. Alone for now, but some day not alone, and still this alive. I hope.

Thursday, 23rd June, 2011.

son threw up in the toilet; the orange stuff was just soup

So it was soup that made me almost go arse-over as I stepped across the floor. I was confused when I regained my balance, wincing at my already-sore pulled back muscles, not quite able to recognise what it was. I forgot that I'd taken pumpkin soup out of the freezer and left it on the bench.

My first thought was that perhaps First-Born had come home drunk and thrown up. I followed the soup across the floor and up the side of the fabric couch, as though it was a series of footprints that had to be tracked. And then I turned around and saw the broken container on the bench and realised what it was.

I wondered why – having been teaching for hours – both of my children had gone their separate ways and just left it there for me to slip in and then clean up. But that's beside the point. When Son emerged and told me he threw up it confused me again. I looked at the soup, I looked at him, and he said *'Not that'*.

He'd had a middle-ear imbalance because he got water in his surgeried ear. Room spun, he fell against the wall, got more dizzy, ran to the toilet and chucked.

Big question mark issuing from my head, finger pointing at the floor. *Wha...?*

Turns out it was First-Born. They threw the soup, they went into my room and threw the chair and my washing basket around and then emptied most of the contents of one of my cupboards all over the room. Then they said *'Now we're even'*.

Why we're allegedly even is that I had to empty a big travel bag that I lent them over a year ago, so that Son could use it for his Central Australia trip with school. He asked them for it, they took too long. They haven't spoken to me all week and made it quite clear I'm not allowed to speak to them.

So I went into First-Born's room, found the bag underneath stuff on the floor, and I carefully and respectfully placed the contents of the bag onto their bed, so that their things wouldn't be stepped on when they entered the room. I wasn't doing anything mean, I was just doing what needed to be done. Then I left the room and wiped the bag clean, it being in a better state than I'd expected it to be. I left it to air out, picked Son up from school, and took him holiday shopping.

I bought a sleeping bag. I bought him socks and a beanie and thermals and a coat that he loves because it's left-of-centre. Son and I laughed as we shopped – it was the first time I've spent with him in weeks and weeks, because he shuts himself away so much. It was, before I slipped in the soup, a very good day.

We're not even. First-Born's way ahead of me. They're already sleeping, for instance. I've cleaned up most of the soup. Now I have to clean up the mess in my bedroom, and won't be able to sleep for a long while yet.

So. What does giving up look like, I wonder. Or do I already know.

Saturday, 25th June, 2011.

Bon Voyage

I did it. I managed to see Son off on the bus. He was so happy, and I felt like a stranger watching through the window as he talked to his friends. It was dark so it didn't matter if I cried. I was standing alone anyway. All of the other parents were talking to each other, excited, with obvious social histories that I don't share. I don't know how they do it, and wonder if that's just another failing of mine.

Anyway, Son was happy, that's the main thing. I held my notebook, desperate to draw his profile, because I forgot to photograph him on profile – those amazing features, the shadows. I want to draw him. The portrait I've painted is front-on. And no I'm not an obsessive mother. He's independent, and I let him go where he needs to go. But I watched him through that window, and thought of going home to this place that's just a corpse of what was once a real home. I thought as usual about my failings as a parent. To provide a good life.

That I managed to get him to the Central trip is a big deal. It means more than anything that the life I give him is normal, and happy. And that I don't show how much I'm disintegrating inside.

The house symbolises everything. I wrote a story about it that I need to send off, but there's more to it than that. I've realised over the past few days that I'm very, very depressed. I function so slowly, that's the tip off. I didn't think I was, because I still have strong ideas and seem to have the impetus to keep going. But when it comes to doing the things I do, I don't enjoy or see the point of anything much. Certainly not of doing things.

I can't even articulate right now. I don't like the label or the fact of depression, as though it's this big and all-consuming thing. If there's an excuse to be happy I'll find it. But now, the sense of loss is so overwhelming. Mourning, grieving, like the counsellor said. I need to feed it into art, which I am doing in theory. Keep pushing.

The only time I reached an extreme low was years ago. I was so truly convinced that my kids were better off without me, that I was ruining their lives by existing, that they'd be better off if I was dead. I can't remember how I pushed past that point last time – I just remember not talking to anybody for ages, the way I don't now, and then one day making a desperate phone call to Friend W-L to ask for help, or just to talk.

But now there's nobody I want to have that conversation with. Right now I don't want to die, but I don't want to live, either. Or I do but I can't find a way to love living. I used to be so full of life, and I know it's the absence of hope that's doing this.

Anyway, misery is revolting to write about. It's just, I think I was right to think that back then. My kids really would have been better off without me. Everybody would.

So I don't want to die – emphasising that point – but I know that suicides don't talk to people. That it's easy to just keep it inside (this sadness) and not express it to anybody. That silence is dangerous. That the people who don't talk are the ones who aren't safe from themselves.

I don't want to be that person. I told myself years ago that if circumstances ever got so bad or wore me down this much I'd ask for uppers, or just use illegal drugs. Two things I never want to have to do. I was always so proud of being so happy, as though I had the answer to everybody's emotional struggle and could help them if they asked me. Now I don't believe in any of it.

Son used to be so social but now never asks for friends over = this house is so empty of love. What am I really giving him? First-Born hates me. They told him they're going away while he's on holiday because they don't want to be here alone with me.

How do you feel good when you know that? When you love them both so much but can't reach either of them, albeit = different kinds of distances.

So what am I. Am I depressed? Or just too alone? I thought when First-Born came back that it wouldn't be perfect, but that the bad phase would become a memory of things absolved by the goodness to come.

I don't know why I'm trying to work out the difference between sadness and depression, when in reality I know the answer to that already. Sadness is sadness, unhappiness, whatever you want to call it. Depression is when the sadness won't end, and you can't imagine it ever ending, or you need to undo it but know that it can never be undone.

For now = be happy that Son's having the time of his life. And sad for the contrast, because I can't give him that here. All life is elsewhere. I have two weeks to fix it. I need to not-be so broken. [Shit.]

Taiko today. One morning with my friends and I'll be so happy. Which is where the answer is = just socialise constantly. Be where you're alive so that you end up being more alive than dead inside. Don't stop moving.

Wednesday, 29th June, 2011.

It's not First-Born's fault. Most of the behaviour comes from a form of self-loathing. They're just frustrated. Doesn't help me at all that I know this. Not in my everydayness. I'm not strong anymore, in fact I'm an emotional wreck, bordering on sadness all the time. Blah blah blah. Push past it. Just push until we're all safely on the other side.

Thursday, 30th June, 2011.

These Days

The empty nest thing is real. First-Born's been away for a few days, and I can imagine now what it must be like to only have to care for myself. I'm not very good at it. I've been craving apples and grapes, but after days and days have only just now gone to the fruit shop. The singing fruiterer wasn't there, but even in his absence he's a great supplier of grapes. I bought too many for one person. This aloneness would take getting used to, I think.

Today I've been in the garden and that means I've been in the sun. Time spent doing, not creating – just maintaining the world against its own rampantness. Freeing unhappy plants from the cloying creeper weeds. Hard to pull from at the root, but tug at them gently and they come towards you like rope. I made rope out of some of them. Found, beneath the creeper that I usually allow to remain on the fence, that the broken fence is partly made from a rusty old metal bed base. Like real farm junk, and that made me happy. Logs and bits of other people's history.

It's taken me a long time to face the garden because I don't like to be watched, and down there I'm so visible. Today my hair's long and wild, so wild I couldn't see what I was doing. And I remember that summer when I loved the garden, and thought about how it didn't become the artist's book I'd planned, though some of the notes I wrote made it into a story I just recently tidied up.

Everything goes somewhere.

So I freed the pond, shredding my fingers on rose prickles because I couldn't find my gloves. Get yer stinking tendrils outa my water. It was the pond that drove me down there.

I had a story in my head. Not one important enough to actually write yet. But it was a nice day. Thank fuck it's been so sunny for so long. Lots of time reading in the sun by the window.

Anyway, that's who I am without my kids here. This is how quiet life will be when they grow up and out. As long as they're happy, I can be too. What's left of me.

First-Born's home now. Not noisy, but not friendly. The smell of cigarette smoke mixed with perfumes. I knew they were home when I came upstairs because the screen door was open, and I could smell them as I came inside. Lucky I bought such a big bag of grapes after all.

July 2011

Friday, 1st July, 2011.

Nothin' Up My Sleeve...
In this peace I can contemplate the feared writing of a story. Because today I spent a good hour or more with my pitchfork, stripping the vegie garden of its weeds. By morning I'll have covered it in weed mat, and it'll stay tidy for the rest of winter. Strange that the satisfaction comes from making it unusable, but still. Somehow now just the act itself is nice.

Anyway, the stories. Have been writing. Reading mostly, but writing. The wall I've hit is a bastard thing. I have these stories in my head, and this weekend I'm going to make myself turn them into small worlds. It doesn't matter if they're shit – I'm happy to write bad stories if I must, just to get that world-making thing into practise. Haven't constructed a whole new universe for a while, and it's about time I did.

Not to sound too grandiose or nothin', but I'm sure if dog-spelt-backwards existed he'd have said something similar on the eve of that Monday. [Hah!]

Monday, 4th July, 2011.

Incredibly, No Less
Not-Named-Yet Friend was over for dinner before we went to a concert last night and asked to see my paintings. I sighed and thought *oh okay*, knowing I haven't done much worth showing, and that the one I have done recently is so mechanically rendered it's ordinary.

I showed her some, and pulled others out of plan drawers and painting racks, but not far enough out for her to really see them properly, because I was embarrassed. By the emptiness of my practice.

I have to earn the right to show anybody anything by starting again, and producing the stuff trapped in my head.

She later sent me a message through F@ceb**k, and it was warm. Except, she said in passing that I was *'incredibly gifted'*. I never know what to say to that. Gee thanks? It makes me uncomfortable, and emphasises the emptiness for me. Skill is nothing without cohesive thought, and without context, and the ability to communicate something that really speaks to the world you're in, in a language that the contemporary world will appreciate. So I'm not gifted, no. Just lost. Incredibly lost.

———

I wonder what'll happen if I ever get my shit together. If suddenly all of these things I do – which are all over the place, and mostly stagnant in practise despite being active in theory – eventuate and become ready to be put out there. Imagine that. So many of them.

———

Tuesday, 5th July, 2011.

So – Reading.

Last night was the first night since my newfound peace was, um, found, that I've gone to bed without a book to read. How weird is it, that after so long without reading properly, I finally start reading the way I used to read, like really really reading, and suddenly I can't stand to be without a book.

This is a lesson in greed, sort of. Because I get them, I read them, I can't stop reading them, and then they're gone. Why I don't have indigestion I don't know, but I really need to pace myself.

It's just – fuck. What I've been missing. Thank goodness it's back

I read *The Zookeeper's War*, Steven Conte, figuring that prize winners are a good place to start. Even though enough with the war already, yah? Still, I'm in love with words again.

One small passage where I flinched: *'When the war's over, the rest of Europe will tear Germany apart, and what's more we'll deserve it...'* (page 117). Part of a prescient sentiment that can only create scepticism regarding the story's authenticity. Please don't do that – putting today's regrets into yesterday's minds, even if you've found some sort of evidence that those prescient regrets were there at the time... just don't.

After that, so swept away. I want to grab his face and kiss his cheeks, because of what he's given back to me. The first time since forever that I've really been able to live inside something.

And then *The Tiger's Wife*, Tèa Obreht. So beautiful. Not just so beautiful; it's rich and mesmerising. Unique, imaginative qualities I don't have time to describe. This one's a keeper. How is she only twenty-five years old? How the fuck? Two faces to grab and kiss. I hope she has a bodyguard, because I think everybody must react that way.

And here's something interesting – there are three books out there that describe the fate of zoos during war. (The other one is *The Zoo Keeper's Wife*, which I haven't read.) Actually, four; I first came across the consideration of zoos and animals during war in *The Wind Up Bird Chronicle*, Haruki Murakami.

Visible threads of the collective consciousness. Interesting, like I said.

Friday, 8th July, 2011.

A Something of One's Own

I'm really good at the room-of-one's-own thing. I have five rooms of my own. Not because I'm greedy, but because I actually use those rooms and nobody else seems to need them. One's been taken over for storage because I house Ex-Husband's many, many [many many many] things, but it's also where I keep my painting racks and some books. Another is set up with desks but is also so cluttered with storagey things that I use it as a *'walk in, think and then leave with what I need'* space. That's where I keep my most important active research material, and some of my art materials. All neatly arranged for easy access.

The main studio's set up and active. The other downstairs living room (that leads to the studio rooms) is set up here with my desk-top computer and with drawing tables and other desks pushed together to make an inking area, and a wall that hangs works in progress. That's where I work on them if they happen to be large and paper.

Downstairs is all mine; one great big depository for the stuff that helps my brain tick over. We have four cats, and if I wanted to swing all of them down here I could.

So room[s], yes. Head space? Not so much. First-Born's been in all of these headspaces and I haven't worked well for a long time, which feels like such a waste of opportunity because I won't have this much space to myself forever. I know that when we eventually leave here, I'm going to be despot of much smaller spaces. Which means I need to grasp these ones now, bull by the horn. Which means another re-arrangement is due.

It's time to move a desk back into my bedroom. I'm reluctant, because it makes the room so full. And a bugger to vacuum. And because I've been remembering my Golden Age of writing, when I used to have the desk set up in what was then my "work room" but is now my studio, which is essentially the same thing except that I don't want to write in there because I work with oils and don't think I should be breathing them in if I can help it. Even though I don't use a medium. Who knows what'll kill you? Ya know?

I absolutely cannot die until I've finished the things I'm working on, and because by the time that happens I'll have new things I'm working on, I'm not allowed to die any time soon or in the future. Ever, maybe. Say no to paint fumes.

But I loved working in there. I'd get up insanely early and sneak in while everyone was asleep, and have so much quiet. I've done this with a desk in my room before, but it's not the same.

I'm so sick of giving time to the rearrangement of stuff in this house. I seem to have to do it so often. I don't know if I'm restless because of an ineffective arrangement of space, or if the ineffective arrangement of space is a symptom of my restlessness. Both, I suspect.

Managing a household that you work in is one thing if you're on your own, but managing a household you work in is so much harder if you have to manage both the material things and the emotional chaos of other people. Especially when they do nothing to help. Regardless, this time I need to get it really, really right, so I don't have to do this again. House: the Definitive State.

Still Friday, 8th July, 2011.

Reading Again

The most gentle Book. I'd been running on four hours and then three hours of sleep respectively, for two days in a row. Insomnia again. At first because First-Born woke me at 3:05 am when they came home, and then the next night because I woke spontaneously at 2:30 am. I think my body, after many months of middle-of-night wakings, doesn't trust that it's allowed to sleep.

Plus I've been getting up at zero o'clock, so my body thought why bother going back to sleep? I've wanted to get up at 4 am, and now I do.

Instead of collapsing last night I went out to pub trivia with my neighbours. (We didn't win this time, but we might've come close if Old Guy hadn't been holding the pen and insisting on putting *pig* where the answer was [so obviously] *chimpanzee*.)

I like my neighbours. It's weird though, because I'll never fit into their broader husband-wife social group. All of the pub people (it's a very clean, hillsy kind of pub/restaurant, local) kiss each other hello and know each other by name and have a history. They all get excited about the sports page of the trivia, to which I know not a single answer. Not one. Also, they do mystery weekend tours together, visiting wineries interstate and having general couple-y countryside fun.

So this is what I'm missing by being so pertinently single. And poor.

Anyways, I'm digressing. Before I went out I crawled into bed with the electric blanket on (it's freezing), but instead of sleeping I read some more of Gerbrand Bakker's *The Twin*. When I got home later I did the same. And that's probably why I'm not really digressing at all – the whole novel's about a very calm and pertinently single guy that I shouldn't relate to but I do. I think I married this guy, or someone very like him. Which should put me off, given that I also separated from him.

But no, I find him very addictive. Even though it's strange because it is after all fiction, and having met quite a few Dutch people (GENERALISATION ALERT) I didn't think fiction was something they were capable of writing. The ones I know have a characteristic inability to use their imagination. If they in fact even have one [!!]. I picked it up because I'm so fond of one of my students, who happens to be Dutch. I'm looking for samenesses and not finding them.

Also beside the point. The point is that the novel describes such a tiny world, and that in itself is extraordinary in a world this big. I don't need to read this one quickly, it's not that kind of story. I just like being in his head, even when I'm still slightly drunk and should be sleeping. Even now, when I should be painting, I want to go back to it. Only discipline makes me wait. So maybe I do need to read this one quickly. Sleep be damned.

Saturday, 9th July, 2011.

Homecoming

Sometimes you just look at your kids and think *'Wow – I made them'*. And then you think *'!!!!!'*.

It's not that I was counting the minutes 'til Son got home from Central, but this morning went very, very slowly. I know this because I looked at the clock a lot. About every minute or so.

The thing about your kids is they're customised to fit into your life just-so. It's very nice. This morning First-Born gave me a block of chocolate with *'I [heart] Mum'* on it, the sort of thing they used to do when they were little. It's so sucky it's hilarious. And Son dug in his bag to find me a present he bought, which was my name and a tiny smiley face printed on a grain of rice floating in oil inside a love-heart that I need to hang on a strap of leather and wear around my neck.

First-Born and I stared at him because he seems different, kinda grown up, and has let his bum fluff [facial hair] grow over his lovely bone structure. He's so cool when we stand there discussing his nice, masculine jawline in front of him, and both of them say such funny things. I really do stand there thinking *'Wow – I made them'*, and *'!!!!'*.

Then Son read his school report and said *'Heh – I'm awesome'* before walking off to the shower. (I'm awesome too; I got 95% for theory. Particularly hard to please teacher. Just puttin' that out there.)

They make me larf. We make a good family, the bare bones of us. I like today. [Happy!]

p.s. Son did qualify that he bought me a present because everybody else was buying a present for their mothers, so it seemed like the thing to do. Don't take it too seriously, Mothah. I even find *that* funny.

Thursday, 14th July, 2011.

That Were Dumb

I was talking to Young Hermit Friend about art and writing and associated whatnots, and we got onto the subject of needing to be suddenly rich. She reminded me that I was supposed to publish a best seller to achieve this. Which of course is never gonna happen, but it did remind me of one of my manuscripts, which I happened to have worked on during the dark days of summer. And which I promptly forgot about.

How do you FORGET you've tidied up a manuscript? How do you be excited about writing something one day, and then forget the thing entirely the next?

After talking to her I opened the files and started reading. And I discovered that I really had tidied it up. I read it and started laughing, possibly a little maniacally. And I read on, expecting to find crap somewhere in there, but no, it's okay. Is it publishable? I don't know. As I keep repeating, people used to say it was, but I shelved it because I didn't believe them. So in its cleaner state = is it? Who's gonna know? It's so hard to even have your work read these days.

But anyway. Maybe I should try. I go from stupid to outright ridiculous if I don't even try. And if that doesn't work, it's okay; at least I amuse myself with the thing. If you have something fun to take to the grave with you, maybe that's the modern version of having done okay with your life.

Sunday, 17th July, 2011.

And Then She Remembered the Synopsis

Of all the things I write, I find the synopsis is the thing that breaks me. They're evil things. EVIL. But the thing is done – horribly and inadequately done. Never let it be said that I don't have at least a little bit of discipline.

Now back to art. Because part of the studio was mended, a couple of my unfinished paintings are leaning up against the wardrobe in my bedroom. So when I wake I roll over and see them. And they haunt me. Because of what I can do, because of the visual obsessions I've been thinking about but not acting upon. The form and the colour and potential to make something of them.

Because now I can. I've dropped my midweek shifts at work and suddenly I have undistracted time. This terrifies me, because there's so much to do I don't know where to start.

I don't know why I'm so scared. Am I scared of having my momentum interrupted again and again? I have to overcome this. Without it I'm just plain empty. I need that state of rapture. All sucky n' such, but there ya go. The need is overwhelming.

I'm waking at 4 every morning and my routine's taking shape. Any minute now. Really and truly, it's all coming back.

Friday, 22nd July, 2011.

A Spanner in My Works

I was on a roll, truly. And then Baby Friend (he's twenty, I work with him in the kitchens) finally succeeded in convincing me that I should watch *Game of Thrones*. I tried to warn him that I can't START watching or reading anything lengthy, because if I start I won't be able to stop until I FINISH. I told him that I especially didn't want to watch or read anything GOOD because it would take over my mind with DEMONIC FORCE and I wouldn't get any of my own work done.

So guess who devoted ten hours to the obsession that is *Game of Thrones* this week.

The bad news is that my already slow-moving and tentative art practice ground to a veritable standstill; the good news is that I was able to number an enormous amount of Census forms while I watched (I'm doing contract work, Census collection), so I technically just got paid to watch tv.

The extra good news is that even though it ended on a gimme-more note, and I went about the hungry getting of the *Clash of Kings* audio book (second volume), I think I've been able to wean myself off the obsession. Thanks to my impatience with high-fantasy writing.

Here's what I think: that it's sad when a contemporary writer is a slave to traditional fantasy form. George R.R. Martin lost me at the jousting scene. I love his story making, but think it's better suited to film. His writing style isn't engaging [to me]. As in, not beautiful, or poetic. It's just a bang-bang-bang telling of facts that string together to make up a big number of plots. No distinctive voice. Too many facts are a burden and a distraction, so unless you're willing to watch every stone being laid in the construction of your fantasy world, you're not going to enjoy these books.

I didn't think I could wait a year for the next series, but now I can. And I don't need to listen to the books [yet], so they're not gonna take over my life the way I feared they would. I want to know what happens, but don't wanna subject myself to that amount of detail.

Already I'm back to the drawing board with my art. And I'll be able to resume writing without another author's work messing with my head. I'm *free*.

Sunday, 31st July, 2011.

Oh What a Beautiful Crack o' Dawn

Some horrible smell, I don't know, you'd think I was up way before Industry even woke this morning. Apparently not. But even the smell, which only blew in over one stretch of road as the sun was rising, couldn't ruin today's walk.

I can feel everything changing. It smells like spring, the mornings sound like spring (different birds), I'm awake before the world the way I used to be awake before the world, and I'm thriving. Close not just to happiness, but euphoria.

AND today's going to be sunny, so when I take my aching old body out to deliver Census forms – being part of a thousands-big team of people delivering them things all over the nation – I'm gonna be sunned all over. Then to work in the kitchens, then back to delivering, then to bed EXHAUSTED, then up as early as early and into the studios and so on and so on and so on.

This delivering thing is very hard work, I have to say. Hence the aching, old. But I've re-discovered how social I am. And what a snapshot you get of the world you live in just by meeting people on their doorsteps. I've had the ursine bare-backed man, the dressing-gowned woman, the renovation-ish people, the paranoid elderly, the very lonely elderly, the bogans. And they all live next door to each other, it's bizarre.

Anyways, insanely busy but very focussed. Emerging from a kind of coma. Life is good.

August 2011

Tuesday, 9th August, 2011.

Thwarted

Fucken fuck. I wish my motor tics included the swearing arm of Tourette's right now, so that I could shoot off a powerful string of expletives. (Like not-having verbal Tourette's has ever stopped me.) Although I shouldn't say things like that because what I do have is bad enough and verbal-T people must go through hell.

But anyway, now's not the time to distribute my sympathies elsewhere, when I need them for myself. I recognise this as a full-on shitty mood, something I don't very often experience. I was supposed to paint today, I stayed home so that I could paint uninterrupted. My absence in the studios will no doubt be noted, but the plan was that it'd be okay when suddenly so many works appear impressively close to finished, all at once, in my skool studio space.

Not gonna happen.

Truth is, I'm getting up early, as planned, but I'm not getting any writing done. I'm juggling too many things *again* because I don't ever *learn*. I'm painting, but I'm so busy I'm restless and I'm not getting that uninterrupted time, so I'm behind the schedule I set for myself. Schedule! What was I thinking!

Anyways, shitty. Because I started reading *The Last Werewolf* yesterday (Glen Duncan) and I made the mistake of picking it up "for an hour" before starting in the studio this morning. Hence, no studio. It's just so beautifully written. And why should I fight off the drive to read when reading's a such an important part of writing, and it all ends in the regeneration of words and so on and so on? Responsibilities be damned? Well I'll tell you why, because now it's too late to start painting, and all I can think about are the unstarted and unfinished things. So *many* of them.

I'm feeling quite pathetic. Especially because I should've divided the reading into two anyway. This novel – addictive, utterly – reminds me of something I don't particularly like. If I met a werewolf I'd avoid them because apparently a lot of their thought is devoted to how they "found themselves". Very deep shit, and entertaining to a point, and the novel's not really repetitive but could do with some streamlining of this reflective element. Or just be read in smaller doses than my greedy fat brain has allowed for. My own silly fault.

Truth is I like Jake's reflections, and he shouldn't become the victim of my rare shitty mood. What really shits me is plain old *life*. So I'm revising my plan – finish reading the novel, prepare for tonight's training, prepare notes for writing, eat chocolate. Paint some other time. Make life better and postpone being super-human, as per the original plan, 'til tomorrow.

About that:
I realised as I was sitting under a soft lamp this morning, reading (not painting), that this would be the last day I have at home to myself, because First-Born will finish their course tomorrow. And I enjoyed the quiet for quite a while before apprehension set in. Explains at least part of the bad mood.

Monday, 15th August, 2011.

Cars On The Wall
I was walking around in the dark this morning and I happened to look at my bedroom wall, which held a rectangle of soft light coming in through the window. (It's impossible to find real darkness, even that long before the sun rises.) And on this patch of light I noticed movement; a steady onward stream of light and shadow that I realised had to be coming from a steady onward stream of car headlights. Which is amazing because I'm nowhere near a main road. The view from my bedroom is of the Christmas hills in the distance, and a not-too-visible bit of suburbia in the near distance. But mostly it's trees.

It's bad enough that I can no longer shut the sound of traffic out by closing my windows, but now I can see the cars – which are miles and miles away on the Croydon end of Dorset Road – on my wall.

I can't stand it.

Still Monday, 15th August, 2011.

anyway I'm as restless as all fuck

Suddenly all of that energy I've had for art has been sapped. Have been painting and painting, but by this morning it was all just clumsy fumbling about on the canvas. I started to do the final touch up of a painting in this series that I started over a year ago, and forgot how hard it is to resume something so much later. I have no delicacy in me.

Also, am distracted by Census form collecting, which is every bit as un-fun as you imagine it to be. It takes hours every evening, and will continue to take hours every evening for about another week.

I'm also distracted by my neighbours' bins, which are still in front of my house and still overflow onto my garden. I keep ringing the council and they keep not-dealing with the problem gently, which means I'll have to resort to vigilante methods which are *not* going to be pretty.

I should've gone into the school studios today. I should have at least gone for a swim.

Sunday, 21st August, 2011.

Why...

...does the pharmacy label the Caltrate bottle as $11.99, when $11.99 doesn't exist anymore? The transparent manipulation of people. Commerce shits me.

September 2011

Friday, 9th September, 2011.

clearly i've been very busy
well, duh. so busy that i haven't read any other blogs recently, not even my favourite. but i read her just now, a conversation between her and her son, and it made me incredibly happy. it's nice that a child you've never met can make you smile so big. and what a lovely bit of nice to end my day on.

10th September, 2011.

A First Time
For the first time I picked up an anthology that included two of my stories and started to read. It's not a fancy schmancy anthology, just an award thing, but that's not the point. The point is that I started reading, and because my stories book-end the anthology there was one on the first-ish page. And I didn't hate it. I wrote it so long ago that it was a surprise to me. I read it all the way through, marvelling at the size of my balls while I wrote the thing. Mildly puzzled at how they've shrunk since then.

The whole process came back to me; the idea, the planning, the voice, the fearlessness in making it evolve into a finished piece.

I remember the award ceremony, where actors read the story to an audience. It was the only award ceremony where I felt lonely and unwanted. Because it's not a pretty story, not by a long shot. And nobody told me they loved it, apart from the judge. At every other award ceremony the stories have generated a kind of narrative love. Something warm. But with this one = either it doesn't lend itself to performance (it doesn't), or nobody likes having an impolite raging erection shoved in their face (they don't).

I really did have guts back then. It's making me feel strong remembering. It's making me wanna write with a vengeance.

Wednesday, 14th September, 2011.

Serious Stuff

I have something to get off my chest. As in, I'm rattled. I'm going to get semi-academic here, because the jousting sticks are supposed to be made of rubber but this time I think they weren't. Were they? I don't know.

It's just that I admire this teacher really much. We disagree about a lot of things and have heated discussions in class and them jousting sticks are always poking and jabbing, but it seems to be an okay thing. Neither of us knock the other off of their horse. UNTIL TODAY.

We disagreed about the nature of the PhD in the arts field. We've disagreed before about Writing PhDs; in fact, about Writing courses, for which she has utmost disrespect and isn't afraid to say so. Because you can't *teach* writing n' all that. Which of course is crazy; you can't teach talent (if you wanna define writing drive and aptitude in that way), but you can immerse a writer in a stimulating environment and show them a context in which they can develop, then let them do the work and see what happens. The courses attract people who write (genuine writers) with the promise of community. The writing isn't produced from a vacuum. Not going into that now; suffice to say we let loose on that one.

But when she did the same thing about art school (AT WHICH SHE TEACHES), and promoted what appeared to be a romantic view of art school as a community of artists passing on their artistry, dismissing the value of research to an artist's practice, of course I disagreed. Because there's no single formula for an artist. And I don't know how she could stand there and say that Fine Art PhD candidates aren't doing "real" PhDs, because artists don't do "real" research. I took umbrage, even though I'm not doing a PhD. Because she's insulting the value of alternative forms of knowledge, or alternative structures of research.

Was she suggesting that creative PhDs across the board are tokenistic? Her argument was that we don't need a PhD to be an artist. In fact, to be an artist we need only to produce art.

I argued that some of us want more from art, and see postgraduate research as an opportunity to engage with philosophy and sociology via our medium, using research alongside material that activates thought in an evocative way, that seeks lateral forms of communication that work alongside traditional forms. In other words, that we take the research side of it very seriously and that art isn't just one thing, and artists aren't made from one prototype. For some of us that opportunity is priceless.

She got so angry this time, as though I was disagreeing with her because I didn't understand what she was saying, not because I didn't think what she was saying was right. But seriously, if I did understand what she was saying I think she was making enormous and harmful generalisations, and that they arose from an elitist view of education. Couldn't a scientist make the same disparaging comparison between a scientific research project and an art history research project? (She's a/n historian.) Or a literature project? Anything that deals with qualitative analysis as opposed to quantitative?

She gave a simplistic example, of people learning woodcraft in a woodworking workshop not needing research to be good woodcraftspeople. So I came back with *'So you're saying art is a form of craft that's about product and not engagement with broader culture...',* and so on and so on and so on. I think that's where I started to really get under her skin, and she under mine.

There's nothing wrong with art as a functional craft, but also there's nothing wrong with artists being attracted to research. The two can both fit into this big world, there are no rules, just choices.

My teacher's [allegedly] a product of the purist idea of academia meeting the purist idea of artist and art school. Kind of insults the culture that feeds her. Is that a harsh thing to say? I still admire this teacher. But the academy has always existed, and this is how it's evolving now. The evolution of post-graduate research in all arts fields has elevated the academic status of art as a discourse, enabling us to engage with sociological discussion in a much more proactive way. It's like a golden age for art; and yes there are risks that may lead to exclusion, but if that happens art will fight back. It'll find a way, because that's what it does. New bodies will evolve, the shape of artist communities will change to combat elitism, et cetera.

In the past artists found each other in other ways. The world's too crowded for that type of finding now. This is how we find each other. The ones who want to dig into ideas and politics in a serious way. And on the teaching level, it does make sense to qualify teachers in this way, because it demonstrates their commitment to ideas and their awareness of the wider cultural world in which their students seek to embed themselves.

In this way all types of artists are catered for – those that want to go one way, and those that want to go the other. In the end it's the art itself that will speak with the loudest voice; if the academics don't produce art that speaks to contemporary culture, then they won't last the distance.

Enough. I just needed to say that out loud in this anonymous pocket of nowhere. I feel better already. And I hope she didn't take it personally. I really hope I'm wrong in thinking that this time she did.

Thursday, 15th September, 2011.

Another First Time

I went out to dinner with my Census collector peeps for our thank-fuck-that's-over celebration, and I felt more than a hundred percent comfortable. We said hilarious things and we laughed and laughed and across the table from me were people who looked me in the eye and enjoyed me the way I enjoyed them and it was light and happy and I felt so, so normal.

We all like each other, but with little in common we have no excuses to really see each other much. It's nice to like people for no reason. Just *like* them.

My area supervisor keeps reminding me that I compared the experience to childbirth, in that it's so horrible at the time that you swear you'll never put yourself through it again, but then as soon as it's over you forget, and before you know it you're pregnant again. So in five year's time, who knows. Maybe we'll all still be poor and need the money and sign up to do it again only to realise – too late – that it's such a horrible, horrible job.

Anyway, we have years to not-think about that. For now = I'm glad I can be social again. I've been out a bit recently, but not like this. Not like a human. Maybe this is how it all comes back?

———

Friday, 16th September, 2011.

Anyway There's This Man

I call him "man" in the way a kid looks at a grown up and calls him "man", because he's not a boy or a guy or a person. He's a man, and yes I am the kid and therefore subordinate in a way. A sub-being who can look up to him but not look him in the eye.

So there's this man and I'm way too aware of him. It's shitting me up the wall. The only reason I'm aware of him is that he's around my age, just slightly older, and in all my travels around this small piece of world in which I live, I seldom – if ever – meet people my own age, let alone get thrown into an environment in which they're very, very present.

It starts with awareness. And not good awareness. A week ago I was sure I didn't like him. Really and actively didn't like him. He seemed all intellectual-authoritarian, no-friendliness. But still I was aware of him. Whenever he walked into my periphery my senses were alert. He's ALWAYS walking into my periphery. He's such a THERE person. I'm genuine when I smile and say hello, but also I grit my teeth, think a gentle *fuck off* at him, and then get on with my work.

I know what it is. Being my age he's the measure of things I haven't lived up to. He's the evidence of what I haven't become. As though I failed to grow up. Plus my not-liking him made me think that growing up isn't necessarily a good thing so please stop waving my not-grown-upness in my face, thanksomuch.

Then yesterday all of that shifted, and now his being there shits me even more. Because it turns out I don't dislike him at all. I think he was in a bad mood last week, because this week he was happy and funny and actually I realised I not only like him, but like him quite a lot. And I'm curious about him, which is even worse. The bad thing about that is that I'll never look him in the eye and have an equal conversation, or at least I suspect that won't happen. Not a two-way one. Because I'm the child and I'm subordinate and will not become a grown-up any time soon. There's nothing worse than quite liking the personality of somebody who you can't be equal to.

So now he'll be present and it'll be annoying in a different way. A reminding way, that puts me in my place. Perhaps this is a test. As I grow more and more human, climb more successfully out of the domestic hell-that-was and back into my own skin, I'll know how close I am to human by how easy I find it to have him in the periphery. The less aware I am of him, the more normal I'm becoming. The less self-conscious and self-debasing.

And I have to admit, he makes me work harder to achieve that aim. A challenge I have to rise to. And want to rise to.

Good. Looking at it that way, he's now useful. And I really can put my head down and just get on with my work.

Friday, 23rd September, 2011.

Mortal

I was driving down the main estate street towards Mum and Dad's house, about to pick Mum up to take her to the airport for her Perth trip. I always look for Dad on the street because he walks a lot and is sometimes spottable as a local footpath feature. As I am probably in my own area, even though I try to walk when no one can see me. And even though we don't have any footpaths.

So there I was looking, and I saw this old man not far from the corner of their street. He was hunched over and walking in a strange old-man way. Wearing a hat that could have been one of my dad's hats. It was the hunch that got me – I don't remember my dad ever being stooped like that. So I thought it wasn't him, but then it was him, and I zoomed passed so shocked I almost didn't wave.

And I was suddenly really sad about how old he is. How really old now, deep in his bones. When did he start to stoop forward like that?

We've been talking about books a lot lately (nothing unusual about that, though). When a few of us were together a week or so ago I was talking to Dad and heard one of my sisters turn to the other and say *'They're like Margaret and David, aren't they'*.

Yes we are. And I've been wanting to spend more and more time with both Mum and Dad, wanting life to slow down so that I can, and trying to find excuses to go there. I will do this. More now. Because life's shit and then you die. Fuck.

Sunday, 25th September, 2011.

What to Do About Churchy

I want to smash the angels to pieces. They're not ugly angels, but when Churchy Friend gave them to me for Xmas I didn't know how to take it. She keeps doing that – giving me religious things even though I'm a devout atheist and not into pretty decorative things regardless of their symbolic loading. What the fark will somebody like me do with a large-ish angel ornament? Was it an insult? Was it because she wants something looking over me? Was it supposed to be funny? I wanna smash it real bad.

Anyway, it's sitting here on the computer desk and has been for the good part of a year, since My Epiphany About Churchy Friend. It's here because I got half-way to the smashing but didn't go through with it because I needed to write down WHY before I committed the act. But then I didn't feel like writing about it. Because I didn't know where to start.

And one thing that's stopped me is that she may have seen the two angels as us; two women who just happen to be holding a loveheart between them. The wings on their backs just incidental. That complicates things. Because she loved our friendship and was very generous with her affection. To her it was the ultimate in special.

But still. Smashing. Let's just say we have history, and I thought we were over the garbagey nothings that led her to stop talking to me periodically. Long story short, we're very different and I thought that our differences had ceased to matter. Because I said some confronting things, years ago, and we've been proper friends ever since. I believed that the closeness was very real.

UNTIL. Late last year. She was angry at me for some reason, probably I'd let her down, or let somebody down, as I do so often. Some social thing I didn't make it to. I suck like that, and she gets angry about it. I remember trying to explain to her with a text that things were rough at home, as they were. At the time I was told I should be putting my child through a particular ordeal but I couldn't do it, and therefore had to go through my own ordeal, and cope with all sorts of Really Horrible Emotional Shit.

I kept the text short and to the point, not dwelling, not asking for anything. Just letting Churchy know. This matters a lot, because all the way through those last few months of the year I didn't talk to anybody about what was going on. There was nothing anybody could do, so what was the point? The most I would do was let them know it was rough and then change the subject.

Sob story aside. Churchy Friend, who happens also to be a youth worker, flipped out. Said *she* couldn't cope with this stuff, as in how dare I burden her with my problems. Which I was going out of my way not to burden anybody with. E-mails started, and she can't control herself on e-mail. Says irrevocable things. The past came flooding back, a full-on attack about how I allegedly think I'm superior to her.

It was an awful response to me making a feeble attempt at explaining that I just didn't feel very social at the time. Kicking me in the gut when I was already as down as I'm ever likely to go.

It was, in fact, devastating. Because through that period her normal phonecalls to me – where I didn't mention home at all – were holding me together. She was the only person I bothered talking to, apart from Mum and Dad. I kept calls to my parents brief because they could tell by my voice that I was disappearing. Churchy kept me human just by talking about the world I wasn't participating in. She was a happy thing for me.

The Epiphany, during the course of those e-mails, was that Churchy Friend doesn't like me. Seriously *does not like me*. She loves me because I'm there. And like First-Born, she knows I won't leave her no matter how far she goes with her behaviour. (And as with First-Born, I know that her thinking I have a low opinion of her is actually a symptom of her having a low opinion of herself.)

But that's the thing: I did leave Churchy Friend. As soon as I realised, I was released from the relationship. The burden of loving lifted, and was replaced by a great sense of loss. Because all of that uncomplicated closeness, those years of just plain old enjoying each other, fell away as something that hadn't even been real. And how stupid I, etc. for feeling a pure and uncomplicated love for this complicated human being who actually despises me under her skin.

Churchy kept up the pretence of friendship but I felt nothing, and eventually she learnt to keep a respectful distance. Until recently. When she started to need me again.

Boyfriend breakup. Good, I didn't like him. He was a self-absorbed twat. But now what do I do? For weeks she's been calling and telling me everything the way she used to. That's okay, I guess. I've said supportive stuff with great sincerity. Except that I tell her nothing about my life, and she doesn't ask. Just like it used to be. And she has no idea about how she doesn't even like me. Like she's forgotten.

It's not that I think she needs to be forgiven. It's that there's nothing to forgive; it's simply an awareness that there's no relationship there because she doesn't like me. I loved her. She doesn't like me so much that the one time in my life where she was called upon to just be there – not do anything, just be – she couldn't do it.

So what do I do? Stop answering the phone? Ease her out of this burgeoning habit of needing me again by making myself scarce? I may have to, and I feel cruel. But she fucked up one time too many, and there's no winning me back. Because I've seen the way it really is, and pretending it's otherwise would be like fooling myself into thinking there's a dog-spelt-backwards. Something I just can't do.

―――

Monday, 26th September, 2011.

Automatic Noise Suppression

I realised as I read my local paper this week that I have this built-in to the appropriate region in my brain. Because it occurred to me that every single news page – double spread – had between one eighth and one third of article, and the rest (seven eighths, two thirds) was advertising. That's majority advertising, in case you don't know how to translate a rough ratio. Throughout the whole newspaper, majority advertising and minority [tokenistic] text.

Has it gotten more extreme, or have I just not noticed the extremity before?

In any case it doesn't matter much to me personally, because I don't see the ads. Literally, I turn the pages and my eyes won't even focus on advertising; I see the article and that's it. The rest is a silent haze. I quite love myself for this ability to shut the noise out. Well done, brain.

Now I think I should hardly bother looking at it at all, because the articles are obviously sourced as padding for the paper's real purpose. Such minimal content, and so little concern about local happenings.

I was feeling guilty about not contacting the journalist who left messages on my machine when I won an award last year. I used to do the obligatory articles, but just didn't want attention at the time. And now I'm glad I didn't. Why would you be part of something so shallow. Why would you help them make the world just that little bit more tacky. Such an ugly thing.

Wednesday, 28th September, 2011.

Me Home Town

I photographed Melbourne through the window of my car on Princes Bridge this afternoon. The pre-storm twilight effect gave the city such visual clarity it looked like a model of itself. Then I turned my radio off and tried my best to listen to the thunderstorm as I drove home. Three-thirty in the afternoon and it was so dark I felt like going to bed.

Am I really describing atmospherics in a blog post? For serious? What's really for serious = I've now gone 28 days without chocolate. The two things aren't the least bit related. I'm just saying, is all.

October 2011

Saturday, 1st October, 2011.

Witch-Doctory

I did some research about the chemical composition of happiness. Worried that my outrageously optimistic outlook wasn't returning quickly enough, and wondering why I couldn't feel happiness in that sharp way I used to feel it *every single day*. I was considering uppers as a temporary way to boost myself back to normal, because my brain had just forgotten how to be happy. But I can't stand the idea of them, and keep the possibility only as a desperate measure that I probably won't ever have to resort to.

Turns out I was right about the brain forgetting. Sort of. When you've been through prolonged stress you lose the ready ability to produce serotonin. And uppers won't help you, so thank goodness I didn't try them. Instead it's better to try to boost your diet with tryptophan rich foods, so that you can produce your own serotonin and re-train your brain to be serotoninishly trigger-happy.

But then when I looked at tryptophan sources I discovered that I already eat them by the bucket load. Bananas, every day; avocado, every day; chicken, often; chocolate, every day (well, back then; I'm now one day into my second month without the stuff). And eggs, yes yes yes. So I ordered L-Tryptophan pills on-line, because you can't buy them in Australia. And they arrived, but I can't tell if they're working or not.

I don't think they are. Not yet. Maybe they take a while. But full and sustained happiness impending, any day now. Waiting. Waiting. Waiting.

p.s. Something alarming = on-line products seem to be exempt from source information. The bottle names the distributor but not the producer; the company's international so I don't know where they were shipped from. In fact, there doesn't seem to be a traceable entity to deal with, just an ethereal mail-order body that floats around and offers no accountability. (Duped?)

Thursday, 6th October, 2011.

wot i saw

Although I think being confronted is good for people, and would usually spoon confronting material to my friends like a granny spooning doses of cod liver oil into the resistant little mouths of children, I didn't ask anybody to see *Project Nim* with me this week. I went by my lonesome and gosh it's a sad thing, but so cleverly put together to expose the selfishness of some of the experiment's protagonists. Something to think about for a while, and lament, and then act upon in some indirect way.

I saved the inviting-of-friends up for *The Cave of Forgotten Dreams,* and had to explain what it was so that the suckiness of the title didn't put them off. Although it probably doesn't put other people off, just me. Because I'm hard-nosed that way. Righteously. Because do we know that cave people were dreamy, really? Do we? No. We don't. I stand by my hard-nosedness.

About that title: I'm allowed to be critical because I loved the film and have nice things to say about it. But Herzog really is a suck. He gets carried away with his romantic notions, which are kinda coloured by his awe. I'm not sure if this is cute or annoying.

Something *very* annoying happened when he insisted that everybody in the cave be silent so that they could listen to the sound of the cave (or silence of the cave), and then after about five seconds of sharing that lovely silence with us – his silence-appreciating audience – he filled it with noise. First a fake heartbeat (he'd made some comment about wanting to hear his own heartbeat beforehand), and then with music.

From that point on I was disappointed with the soundtrack, because I was too aware of the silence he wasn't letting me experience. He selected sometimes discordant music, and sometimes classically harmonious music, and it detracted from the impact of the space itself.

Which is such a pity, and such a product of this insanely noisy world we're in. Sometimes music, that wonderful thing, is just inappropriate, and unnecessary.

Anyways, it's a beautiful film, clumsiness of the 3D format notwithstanding. You can really tell it's early days; that 3D technology is just a chubby-legged infant taking its first steps. Despite that, it was a good choice of filming technique, one that really enhanced the volume of the cave interior, which therefore enhanced the nature of the art work because it travels around curves and corners. And Herzog made good artistic decisions about using light and shadow to enhance the volume of the space even more.

Overall the contextualisation and documentary information was well developed. And the post-script about the local nuclear plant – fantastic. And alarming. Finishing with the comment about our crocodile meeting its ancestor-crocodile, though? Herzog, please. Thou art carried away with thyself. Get a grip.

We're so lucky to have Herzog in the world, because look where he took us. Why would you choose any other time to be alive?

Afterthought

Long conversation with Son when I got home, deep into the early hours of the morning. Where I learned more about how pragmatic he is. To such rational extremes. I'm much more emotionally driven than Son is, and yet here I am baulking at romanticism because I prefer a more pragmatic form of understanding. Because to romanticise is to embellish unnecessarily. Perhaps I shouldn't wonder where Son gets it from.

Friday, 21st October, 2011.

Reunited

Chocolate and I. We separated for fifty days, and I could have gone without for much longer. In fact, I didn't even want it. I announced how many days had passed every afternoon in the studio, and every time I did so I marvelled at the number, and then at the utter pointlessness of my amazing feat. And I started to forget why I'd given it up in the first place. (Which is, because I wanted to love food again. I don't love anything. That's just weird.) Because I know that chocolate's good for you. I was living proof of that little fact.

So Day Fifty-One, I've eaten chocolate. I was going to go all the way 'til Xmas, but that would've been plain old dumb. Because what if those tryptophan tablets I've been taking are only counteracting my lack of tryptophanic chocolate? I'm so close to full happiness that chocolate could be the thing that tips me into happiness surplus.

Gosh, chocolate's a bit nice, isn't it? What on earth was I thinking?

Sunday, 23rd October, 2011.

Still Saturday

It's late because in order to avoid the work I'd set for myself, I went to see two movies tonight. Also so that I could be not-home, because home is filthy, because I'm on strike [again] and the kids don't seem to care about the state of the kitchen. Perhaps I'll explain that later; suffice to say I'm trying to shame them into doing me a kindness and it's not working.

Anyway, while avoiding art all day I was cleaning up my work space downstairs; lots of clay dust, and lumps of clay. These reminded me of the hilarity that is art school. No matter who it is (students, teachers), we talk in my studio and eventually they pick up a lump of nothing that's sitting on the end of the table next to my work, and they get excited n' say *'Oh what's this?'*. Every single time I have to explain to them that it's not, in fact, anything. It's just a lump of clay.

I don't know why I'm working so hard, when the not-work I leave lying around on the table is so popular. I could just not-work like that forever and see what happens.

Tuesday, 25th October, 2011.

How I Have Time For Any of This I Don't Know

I wonder why nobody's complaining about the ugliness of the human body when it appears on television with techno magnification. And in the movies, for that matter, but I'm thinking of *The Slap*, really. It's distracting, this gawping into a person's pores. If humans don't look quite so ugly in real life (and actually, they don't), then technology isn't doing us any favours by being so very clever.

On that subject, I watched Christos Tsiolkas being interviewed and he wasn't what I was expecting. I think I've fallen in friend-love with him without even meeting. I don't know what I was expecting, exactly. Somebody a bit more alpha-male-ish? Certainly not such a beautifully spoken somebody. I'm gonna have to carry him around in my head for a bit.

And force myself to watch the rest of *The Slap*. I don't think I'll make it all the way through the show; I'd rather read the book again. Where the characters can walk through the story without their pores so exposed. It seems darker on tv. Like they're in a world with no light in it. I love that in the written version, but not on the screen.

Maybe I'm more shallow than I think; maybe I think Tv-Land needs to be more full of fluff. Tv's where us reading-people go for fluff-fulfillment. Dark atmospheres and skin blemishes just *do not* belong.

Saturday, 28th October, 2011.

The Opening Cervix-ness of My Character

I don't know how these phrases pop into my head. Blame my horrorscope for calling me '*dilatory*'. I had to consult the dictionary. And then panic, because the word means *inclined to procrastinate*. Which is so true at the moment, only it's not really procrastination, it's more like staring at the wall because I don't want to always have to push so hard. (That so fits the dilating cervix image in my head right now. Sorry.)

Forget dilatory. I couldn't wait to get home to read the horrorscope, even though I don't believe in them, because I needed good news and I needed it in advance. Thank you Lilith! You delivered! I have to quote the thing because it's so damn good:

> *Pisceans, let's face it, can often be dilatory but this week*
> *gives you the determination to see something through*

to satisfying completion. Inner transformation, outer growth and a more promising base for future dealings are all likely if you stay open to self-analysis. You may not be quite the person you thought you were.*

It's assessment week, so you can imagine how perfect those words are to me. The fact that I even care should give you an indication of the degree of desperation. Because I don't want to be assessed, I just want to keep working. Feels way too premature to have people looking at my work. Critically.

Anyway, very good to hear that I am, in fact, somebody else. Finally. Ye gods have sent me a warning and I'm taking heed. Let's just hope next Saturday's horrorscope doesn't say *'Well, you fucked that up, didn't you'*.

———

Tuesday, 31st October, 2011.

Once Upon a Time There Was a Brick

There's a note in my file telling myself to write *'the brick story'*. What brick story? Did I have an idea for a story about bricks? How could I have an idea like that and just forget about it so completely? Seriously, how? That's not how my mind works. Where's the lingering shadow of the idea?

———

* *The Leader* newspaper (local)? *The Saturday Age*?

November 2011

Monday, 6th November, 2011.

Where oh Where is Ramona?
I miss her. I've been listening to *The Book Show* podcasts and it's just not the same. Some of the new presenters are on speech steroids; they ask their questions in bang-bang-bang fashion. If not for the deep timbre of words I'd think the audio had been sped up chipmunk-style.

Ramona, Ramona. The newbies don't seem to sink into the interviews the way Ramona did, with pondering and reaction and spontaneity. I get the impression everything's mapped out to the millisecond:

> *hiwhydidyouwritethisbookthanksforcominginthat's allwehavetimefortodaygoodbye*

I'm a-grieving. I don't want this piece of the world to change.

Friday, 10th November, 2011.

What the World is Telling me
I've been writing these letters to men, and that's a bit pathetic. My Friend talked me into putting up an internet dating profile. I have no intention of meeting somebody that way, but it seemed like a fun thing to do at the time. Every now and then I look at it with her (she takes it seriously and is out there meeting people) and remember how awful the process seems, and walk away from it again.

But this time I used it. I wrote to three people. The first = so little in common, but he approached me and I thought it was harmless, and the banter was fun even though his answers made me squirm with their bad-writing-ness. I even contemplated the affair he kept asking for, so I could practise being in love. When I found out what he does for a living, though, I put an end to it because of an ideological clash I couldn't stomach. I'm not good at the casual affair thing anyway. Alas.

The second because he was local = I thought it might be good to have a local friend. To do movies with. Turns out he lived in my street when we were kids and he's from the high country town I love, where Me Lovely Mother is from. We would have thrown tennis balls at each other in my backyard when we were young, playing brandy. He speared my brother in the leg. We have a few things in common but not enough, and he can't write for nuts, but I like him. We have that history and happened upon each other, so we have to be friends as grown ups, it's nature's law.

The third = I approached because I was curious and he's already seeing somebody, but he gave very good letter for that short while.

The thing that struck me through this experience is how starved I am for conversation and how hungrily I'm using words. It's not about the men, it's about the letters, and what they can bring out. What a buzz. Except that that's ALL I get out of it. And when Third Man said *'Such clever words need to belong somewhere I think'* I sat back and thought faaaark. What am I doing? These are just letters – playful but ultimately pointless, and a little vacuous.

Write, dammit. Not to them. My head's so alive with it. So I'm getting the message loud and clear; am disabling those stupid profiles. Looks like the only love affair I'll be having is with paper and a pen.

Monday, 14th November, 2011.

The Penultimate Feed

I went to a book shop and bought so many books the cashier asked me if I was doing my Xmas shopping. As if I'd be that generous. Made me wonder if there's something wrong with buying that many books for yourself. Is there?

One of those books was Isobelle Carmody's *The Sending*, which I've only been waiting for since *forever*. And I discovered that instead of being the last in the *Obernewtyn* series it's now the second-last, and I have to wait until next year to get to the end of things.

I was going to be impatient about it, but as I started reading I couldn't help appreciating how complex a world she's created. That must have taken years (well it did, didn't it), so I shouldn't be mean and want everything now.

A nice story to be allowed to bury myself in, and if I've lost a few days as a result of said burying then that's okay.

It's interesting that there are so many different types of storytellers, and so many levels to reading and writing. By that I'm referring to elements of narrative, language, beauty, cleverness, and so on. High fantasy is usually purely plot driven and expansive in story detail. So I'm not being critical when I say that Carmody's writing isn't beautiful, or clever. It's a clean telling of story. In the whole fat book there was only one line that I thought was beautiful, and it was this, on page 687, describing the line that delineates tainted ground from sand/dessert;

> *'It was impossible to imagine whatever had befallen these lands had not been of human doing, for nature did not cut its cloth so neat.'*

So beautiful. As a whole I'm not sure about this novel; it reminded me of Tolkien, *LOTR,* which I described in an email today as having chapter after chapter of travelling, where you walk across one mountain and look around, then walk across another mountain and look around, and then *whoa!* Another mountain! So it's a good thing the plot already had me hooked. If I were writing it I'd have done that very differently, and perhaps not split the book into two. As a writer who didn't write it, though, and remembering that she's the successful one, I'll just learn from that.

Something to think about while I wait for the rest of the story. And wait. And wait. And wait...

Friday, 18th November, 2011.

Notifications Pending

I get reminders begging me to visit even if I've already been on recently. Like Facebook is this cloying friend who just won't stop ringing me.

It says: *You have missed some popular stories*. Seriously, Facebook? Do you even know what a story is? Because you're not doing an awful lot to tempt me onto your site. *'So-n-so likes so-n-so's photo'*, and *'Another so-n-so likes another so-n-so's status'*, does not a story make.

I hate the email reminders. If I haven't been on it's because I don't want to go on. And those "stories" are the reason why I feel soiled after I *have* been on, the sheer emptiness of days on that site. The sheer desperation in people and their need for constant contact. There are a million gazillion other people in the world; if you want the world to visit you then invite *them* home for lunch and leave me alone.

Saturday, 19th November, 2011.

Le Banyule

It really is like hard core drugs, this art business. It ruins you for the world. You need art and writing and whatever it is that absorbs you, until you can't be happy without them. The more you take, the more you need. Your whole life becomes about challenge and stimulus, and then they stop making you happy, because the more they separate you from the world the harder general happiness is to find. Plus you see through too much because you look at everything through layers of genesis and process and production before you even settle on the artefact.

I met up with friends and went to see the *Banyule Works on Paper* exhibition, which I did love doing and I always love doing, but ya know? I wasn't moved. I used to be moved. What's happened to me that I'm not moved anymore? There are some beautiful pieces, but they weren't enough.

I hope it's just because I was viewing them out of context. My biggest fear is that I'm turning into the teachers (oh please no), who seem to be immune to most art. Who've scoffed so much art into their systems they need a really sharp hit to give them even a vague sort of thrill.

I was saying to one teacher, who happens to be able to see that the emperor's often naked, that the other teachers seem bored by art. I don't want that to happen to me. I admire them in other ways, but that immunity to certain aesthetics is disturbing.

So I resolve to keep my head fresh. I think it comes down to how you share it. This is the second time I've said this this week, but I need to repeat it: maybe art school's the worst thing an artist can put themselves through. Such a pity that it's also [allegedly] the best.

Sunday, 20th November, 2011.

to camus or not to camus…?

Sensitive Studio Guy Friend had a page from Camus' *The Outsider* up on his studio wall, and when I read it I was stunned. I thought and thought about it, regretting that I'd avoided reading Camus because of my old Pretentious Philosophy Friend and his stinking elitism. His dropping of Camus' name was on the sickening side, so of course I thought of Camus as male wank fodder that I could do without.

But after reading that page I held it in my mind, and waited for the right moment to savour the book. It was among the pile of books I bought the other day. From reading that one page – the shooting page – I was convinced that the language would transform my mind in some way. Change my life.

Of course there's a *but*. The world would be so good if the transformation of minds happened without buts and clauses. Because I don't think I can finish reading it. That page was better on its own. The flavour of the novel is so depressing, and perhaps not a good thing for somebody so newly returned to happiness to be reading. The parallel of event without emotion, or drive without passion. The passivity of a perpetrator in the face of consequence. And yet that's what it's about, so I do need to finish it. Maybe just not today.

Wednesday, 23rd November, 2011.

A Leopard Can Change Its Spots

Being a socially-inclined introverted person is like having a constant argument in your head about how much to throw yourself out into the world. But sometimes it comes easily, if the world gives you the right kind of welcome. And yes, that does mean that introversion can sometimes have a lot to do with fear.

So over the past few weeks, to overcome my big-fat-chickenness, I've been socialising all over the place. It's weird, the art school dynamic, which involves socialising in groups. The world is a Facebook, I think I've said that before. When you speak to one person you speak to everybody. And that's good, it means you become part of a crowd – more than one crowd – and belong in a kind of hive.

But there's the other kind of social and that's the one I'm craving. So yesterday, with pent up readiness for writing, when I told myself I was going to write up the poem idea that occurred to me last week and then did so, I was so happy that I sent it to a new-ish friend. A fresh piece of work with such immediacy that the private act of writing became something else entirely. Sharing it felt good, like bringing the poem to life.

The writing felt good, too. More natural, less self-conscious. A very fluent few hours of pure and blissful concentration. All language and beat. This matters because I've been wondering if I actually have poetry in me anymore, if maybe I'm a prose-writer with poetic leanings and poetry just ain't my thing. But that friend wrote back to me straight away to say *'Loved the poem. Absolutely loved it. Beautiful sparse language, chilling and powerful'*. [!!]

Having heard from Old Teacher that day, I also sent it to him, because he likes poetry and words and we kinda meet on that level, and I needed some reassurance about the musicality of the thing, so asked him if it worked. He wrote back with *'I think it's an amazing poem. Its "musicality" is of an incantation, obsessive and claustrophobic and erotic.'* (Erotic? Okay so that bit surprised me.) Anyway, this is nice feedback for an afraid person to receive. I've never been more relieved. But most importantly I feel un-alone, and it's made me re-think how I do things.

The New-ish Friend = I've seen a bit of her lately, because I courageously asked her to exhibit with me. The idea of asking this of somebody was terrifying, and I was scared she'd say no. But it turns out I'm respected in my little art world after all. We've met up to do reconnaissance, we've plotted and planned. I've been writing up titles and blurbs and sending them, and polishing up the application, and today she said *'I'm learning a lot from you'*, which is just hilarious because I have NO idea what I'm doing.

But anyway. Very grown up, very social, sharing poetry and composing an exhibition proposal for the Real World. Not such a chicken anymore. Maybe even just a normal person going about their normal business. Feels good to be this busy, and to not be busy alone. If I can keep this up I'll fulfill my ambition of being Somebody Else in no time. Somebody Better. I hope.

Saturday, 26th November, 2011.

On Not Having Shrunk After All

I've been walking around under the impression that I cut a fine figure at 172 cm tall. That's what I thought five foot seven was: 172 cm. It's a number I like very much. It's grown on me and has, in fact, been me.

But last night I stupidly thought it'd be a good idea to measure myself to see if I'd shrunk, curious about when we start to shrink. Being forty-two n' all, I thought I should probably have started by now. Shrinking.

But when I measured myself I was 166 cm. I double triple and quadruple checked by measuring my height again and again, and then asking Son to measure me, and still I was 166 cm. And I was distressed because I thought I'd shrunk 6 cm and at that rate I'd be a midget before I'm fifty. Instead of average height I was now below average. I thought.

But then when I was lying in bed worrying about this thing, I realised I'd read that 166 is five foot six and a half, and I realised that five foot seven couldn't possibly be 172 cm so it's all a matter of misconception. Measured myself again just then and I'm almost 169 cm, smack bang on five foot seven, exactly where I was all the time.

No shrinking! I'm still young!! Now I just have to get used to being a whole new number. 168 and a bit. 168 and a bit. 168 and a bit.....

Still Saturday.

On Not Falling in Love

Having proven itself useful so far, I was ready for my horrorscope to tell me I'd fall in love this week. It's time. Had an outrageously happy week, full of exhibition openings and glasses of wine and swigs of wine from bottles and perhaps the tiny sharing of special herbs in the middle of the night.

Then there was the writing of the poetry [!!!] and the compiling of the exhibition proposal [!!!] and then it was Friday and I found myself having done all of these eventful things, but sitting at home alone again, where I always am, and I realised that my recipe for happiness requires a more regular pinch of people.

Now that things are getting happier at home, and I'm productive again, I think it's a fair thing to ask of ye gods. I stopped taking the tryptophan and I'm still happy so I know it's all my own doing, pure home-grown serotonin. Perfect for the falling-in of love.

So when my horrorscope told me there'd be mixed or missed messages I have to say I was disappointed. How can I work with mixed messages? Why can't men just communicate properly? No, this won't do at all. Can I change what's written in the stars? I'm a writer, can't I just write my own stars?

Oh well. It's raining so the pool will be empty and that means a nice, solitary swim, and a nice solitary sauna, and then home for some nice, solitary drawing (which is actually something I'm enjoying right now). And then it'll be Saturday night. I could organise a movie with friends. It ain't falling in love, but I suppose it'll do for now.

Sunday, 27th November, 2011.

Deep Personal Shiz

Turns out I didn't do the movies with friends. Turns out I had my lovely long swim, then I went in to the studios to see the graduate exhibition again, this time more of it, and there were a couple of friends there so I hung with them for a while and we got to talking and Rampant

Woofter Friend told me I seem so joyous lately, full of joy n' such, n' I said *Yes I am, aren't I? So happy.*

I could have arranged movies but I came home and watched one by myself. Then to a family lunch today before work, and it was happy all the way, but now I'm home again and the sadness just hits me. I realised that all of this time I've been spending with people is about being beside them and doing thing after thing after thing, but no sitting down and looking someone in the eye and just "being".

I listened to my kids talking when I got home from a walk tonight. They were discussing their Facebook pictures, because First-Born posted some photos that I took today. Nice photos, only neither of them are Friends with their lovely mother on Facebook so I wasn't tagged or included in any of it, and I realised that even when I'm part of something I'm not part of it at all. Just this invisible person that everybody loves but who's really on the outside of everything. I think you need to be in love to be on the inside of anything, because your partner makes you matter.

So I'm lonely and feeling unloved again. I have to snap out of it. I have to train myself not to need. To not-need. That way I can never be disappointed.

Been looking at old photos, where I was so happy. This is the thing I want back, but how do you just forget that the last few years happened? You can't. I lost so many years, more than three, and I won't ever get them back. They'll always be there, one big fat scar I can't get rid of. First-Born's been good lately, sometimes very good, but when they get that edge in their voice I go backwards again.

I don't want to keep remembering that. It makes me realise that everything is nothing after all. I need somebody to counteract the effect, and to counteract the memories, but I'm needing something I can't have. Seriously, snap out of it. And do what makes you calm; draw, and draw, and draw. The doing of things is what matters. So that when you do snap out of it you'll still have some substance.

Right, then. I'm going to stop needing people, effective as of NOW.

———

December 2011

Sunday, 4th December, 2011.

This Morning...
I'm going to Coincidence Man's house for breakfast. It's nerve-wracking to be going to meet somebody you've never met even though you have actually met them before. The walk from car to door. Dread.

Monday, 5th December, 2011.

Yesterday Morning...
I did indeed go to Coincidence Man's for breakfast. Survived trip from car to door. Was very relaxing, actually. He's nice company. I might have stayed 'til way past lunch time. Had to leave eventually because had to go to work.

Was a very technological visit. My phone going off with texts, his phone ringing, and our conversation punctuated by perusals of internet via laptop, as though all of our dialogue came with illustrations. Very modern. One of those illustrations was of Feral Brother's head. I don't have Feral on Facebook because I keep my distance, so Coincidence Man showed me the profile photo he found when spying on us and he's right, me brother looks like Charles Manson and is therefore one very scary-lookin' fucker.

Anyway, what an interesting day. Just hangin'. What do I think of this, I don't know. He gave me nice paper and a bottle of beautiful, beautiful ink that dries both cool and warm and is therefore freaky and has me obsessed. Ink makes my brain explode, so pleasurable I almost can't stand it.

What else. His friend popped in and I loved watching them together. Something, I don't know. I felt so socially satisfied, sitting there in the middle of their conversation. My conversation, too, but ya know? I wondered how it is that I was there, and how you become part of something that already exists, and will I become part of anything or is this a weird one-off thing. Question mark.

How do people become friends? We'll see. Maybe it starts with breakfast and ink.

Wednesday, 7th December, 2011.

Relief on the One Hand, 5% Dumber on the Other

Or perhaps five percent doesn't cover it. Yesterday I lay down on the balcony to read in the sun and lifted my top so that my tummy was exposed, because I love the heat and was curious about just how much it would burn if I tried to be less cookable, like everybody else. The result of this scientific experiment is that I have a sunburnt tummy. First time that skin has seen colour for a great many years.

Rangadom is a cruel thing.

But anyway, Art Skool results were there when I looked this morning, and I'm so relieved because my studio result could've gone either way. I didn't even submit my paintings, which made up half a semester's work; just presented my more recent work because that's what felt most relevant. I wanted my grade to stay at my studio average or be slightly up, because that's how I feel about where I'm at, at the very beginning of things but on the right track. Had it been less I'd have worried about not having the teachers' respect. Amazingly, given I only felt like I was fully there towards the end, my grade's slightly up, and the message is *Right Track, Keep Going*.

That means I don't have to feel embarrassed or small when I go back. Thank goodness.

But with theory, having worried for most of the semester that I was offending my teacher with my big fat argumentative mouth, my grade went down from 95% to 90%. I put the numbers here to show you how silly it is to be sitting here raising my eyebrows in half-concern, half-amusement. Who's gonna quibble about it when either grade is pretty good? Not me. But I do wonder if the message that number is giving me is that I am in fact five percent less clever, or if I'm five percent more annoying.

My intuition's been telling me it's the latter. Or maybe both. Either way, it's much easier to work your way up than to fall a notch. I was planning on worrying about this all day, but I think if I go off and write and draw I can push it to the back of my mind. Make things in the real world, where grades don't matter but story does.

I always surprise myself when I think such sensible things. But what's the bet I go off into the day and worry anyway.

Friday, 9th December, 2011.

Rectifying an Absence

Upon realising that I have about five seconds left to provide for my kids the way I wanted to, and that I have a weeny bit of excess money in the bank, this week I bought a piano.

Good job, Mother.

I never wanted them to grow up in a house without a piano in it. I don't play. I longed to and begged for it when I was growing up, but my parents were too poor. There were a lot of us. Wasn't allowed to tap dance, either, but that's okay. No bitterness. None. (Churchy Friend has been learning tap dancing for a few years now, and she's forty. Never too late for anything.)

I've probably already mentioned that sometimes when I get home I hear Son teaching himself piano on the keyboard in his room. He had lessons when he was younger but stopped when he had ear surgery. I've always felt bad about not resuming those lessons for him, but life went to hell in a handbasket and years kind of slipped by.

Recently a new violin arrived for First-Born, and when I said *let's buy a piano* they both got excited. Home is now the way it should be. Violin-and-pianoful. Nice.

Saturday, 10th December, 2011.

The Black Plasticking of Things Green

I can't believe that the summer of 2009-10 was only two years ago. Is that even possible? That was the year I spent every dawn and dusk in the garden. It was true love, slipping my fingers into its familiar nooks n' crannies. We got very intimate, my property and I.

I'm not a hippy or anything, but it's all I did, giving myself to the moment and not doing any art whatsoever. I figured that if I put some love into our home and made it welcoming and beautiful my kids would be happier. Because First-Born would stop being angry, on accounta *flowers n' stuff*. Stuff being home grown tomatoes, and all the prettiness, and well why would you be angry with birds singing in the wake of your mother's caring industry?

Nah, it didn't work. So last year Ex-Husband butchered and I let it be. This year I thought I'd do something similar, only this time without sacrificing art and writing. Except, when I started going down there with the best of intentions to make love to the garden, I kinda sado-masochismed it instead.

Am killing the lower lawn with black plastic. Such a good idea I think I'll kill everything. The damn thing's outa control. When I stood out on the balcony late the other night and looked down over the property, I was swept away by the beauty of moonlight glinting offov that black plastic. And by day I look down and imagine that tough, uncuttable grass shrivelling to nothing underneath. I have to say its death pleases me. I haven't let a macabre laugh pass my lips yet, but any day now. *Mwaha.*

Take that, overgrowth. I have a book to write. Art to make. So Nature, you and I need to have a serious talk. I'll still love you, but the affair's over. It's mad passionate maintenance from hereon in. Behave yerself and we'll get along fine.

Tuesday, 13th December, 2011.

Finally, 1Q84

Am blissed out on Haruki Murakami audio. Have put the actual book down and am listening as I draw. And pot about. Can't stop listening, so I'm in a trance.

I think I'm loving the writing bits. And the characterisation. Something to be lost in. Something I can't bring myself to think about out loud.

Although, when it comes to the plot I don't know why Tengo and Fuka-Eri couldn't just team up and be writer-and-ghost-writer, legitimately. I hate to be a party pooper, but surely that would have been okay, and counteracted the need for fraud. Because what a noble thing, to write the story for a dyslexic. If I think too hard about that the plot falls to pieces, and the whole story becomes unnecessary. So I don't think too hard about it. Just enjoy it ignorantly, the way I should.

Hip Hip Hooray

Soon it'll be Other Son's eighteenth birthday, and in the face of First-Born being upset about not being much in his life, I again spend a few thoughts on how bad an Other Mother I actually am.

Partly because Ex-Wife is distant, it just hasn't worked out as a regular extended family thing. Distant in a nice way, but still, her relationships happen primarily in her head. So that she loves us all with great affection, and shows it when she sees us, but doesn't happen to often see us.

Where I'm at fault is, I gave up trying. I let us go with the flow, making suggestions here and there but not following them up when Ex-Wife lets them slide. All because I don't know how to be with them, and have been too scared to try. Because I always assume that I'm not enough, or don't have enough to offer. And I can see that the way Other Son lives his life is very different to how we live ours. Hence my belief in my fundamental inadequacy.

First-Born's right, I should be more proactive. I'll try.

Thursday, 15th December, 2011.

Jettison the Ballast

This internal conflict's out of control. I'm doing too much. I know it, everybody else knows it. And by doing too much I am, effectively, not doing anything at all.

I have to make a conscious effort to limit my projects. Life could be easy if I were to just do one thing. One thing! Why is that so hard? If

I'd just been writing for the last decade, I'd have achieved a great deal. Or if I'd just been doing art, same. But doing both = impossible. Or not impossible if I wasn't studying.

Too much. It doesn't help that these things all have subcategories into which I've stuffed a million projects.

So which ones should I drop? I have to choose. Imagine – life being easy. Really and truly, it could be if I just let a few things go.

Still Thursday.

Close Shave

A phone call from Ex-Wife. Am sensitive to the dark worlds of other people. Can't help comparing them to the clean world of the studios. So what is it that happens outside of that world? These embroilings of other people. An awful way to live, and to waste thought on. Would like to bust her out of the dark loop, but that's never worked before. Some magnetic attraction to dark, psychological drama. Not her fault; our sanity is reliant on the kindness of the people around us. There's an unkind person dragging her down. She responds differently to me. Maybe that's what's hit me. I can't shake her darkness off.

Coincidence Man

My impression is that he likes to be the centre of a vortex and have people come to him. Lives on a main road, waits for people to drop in. Which they do, because all roads lead there.

Interesting, and yet also not. Seems to have so little interest-sharing ability. Another man who offers so little of himself. So easy for me now to opt out. Friendship shouldn't be hard work.

I wish I hadn't received that dark phone call. The sound of thunder I heard just now may have been fireworks. Other people who celebrate. Now the catch up with Ex-W tainted.

Our lives are clean here. Is important and good. Keep busy. Out of sun. social = it will happen the right way, none of this artificial crap. Somewhere in the future.

Friday, 16th December, 2011.

CHRISTOPHER HITCHENS DIED!

oh shit. such a huge loss to the world. irreplaceable. i hope everybody goes out of their way to read God is Not Great. fresh legacy effect. or especially listen to the audio, narrated by he himself with the most beautiful irreverence. much more down to earth and much less engaging in pointless argument than Dawkins.

it made me angry to read the blurb on some footage Ex-Husband sent me, which basically asked if CH would suddenly denounce his atheism when dying (i.e. convert due to fear of death), which is such a fucked-up and ignorant question. death is death and they're just revealing their own awareness that religion primarily performs the role of providing comfort from reality. i.e. they're revealing their own falsity.

i love that he hated the onset of his own death and that he knew what was what. in this case you can say *happy-extinguishment* and mean it in not a mean way. i'm not one to speak aloud about celebrity, but the world will miss him. damn.

Saturday, 17th December, 2011.

Betrayed

By the shade. Because today, at a picnic with my taiko peeps, I got sunburnt even though I didn't set foot into the sunshine.

I should have known that shade isn't really shade, but an artful trick by the sun played on innocent humans.

I might die from this, you realise. Being a ranga and prone to Death by Sun Ray. It's got me very down, and I'm kicking myself for thinking I didn't need to wear a hat. I ALWAYS wear a hat, but this time I wanted to be LIKE EVERYBODY ELSE, everybody else being the people who don't have to wear hats IN THE SHADE. I didn't realise I was letting the sun play such a low-down dirty trick. I'm a summer lover and sun worshipper and pay it so much respect, and still it gets me. Arsehole.

Sunday, 18th December, 2011.

[Sad Content Warning]

A very dark thing, something you don't want to read about so stop reading now.

Too late for me – I can't undo a close friend telling me this today. I can't undo it happening. But here it is: Close Friend went to a farm for a weekend away; she took her dogs; one of her dogs keeps running away, not to escape but because she's a bolter; it's kinda cute but also frustrating; so Close Friend chained her into her ute for the night.

She called to tell me: M the dog. Chained into ute. Jumped out. Chain snagged. Hung herself.

Poor little thing.

I ask myself; had she been my dog, would I have chained her to the back of that ute, or would I have anticipated that happening – the same way I anticipate all of the possible accidents my kids could have when a) crossing the road, b) riding their bikes, c) using fire to cook on the stove top, d) driving a car, e) running down the stairs, and so on – and chained her to something on the ground? When I leave the house I say to my kids:

seeyalater-don'tburnthehousedown-becarefulonthestairs-don'tstickaknifeinthetoaster

Easy to think in retrospect that I would have, and yet we can't anticipate every bad thing, as much as we like to think we're careful. So I can imagine how bad Close Friend feels right now. Because what an awful accident. A split-second thing that ya just want not to have happened. Unbearably sad.

Tuesday, 20th December, 2011.

Finally Final, 1Q84

Thank goodness that's over. It's not often you come across a novel that's a cross between brilliant and monotonous, but Haruki pulled it off. The ending rendered the whole novel pretty much pointless. This could be because I lack grace and subtlety as a person and therefore as a reader, but really, I suspect not. I didn't stop loving the writing bits, and the characterisation, but he sucks at philosophy. And plot. Although he carries it, he doesn't give it a very satisfying destination. Kind of announces a great deal of depth to his characters, but doesn't give them actual depth.

What I love are the simple interactions. But not the simplistic approach to love. True, it's the centre of all things, but that's not enough to sustain a narrative. And there's nothing forgivable about the insubstantiality of that schmaltzy ending.

And what about the loose threads? The final chrysalis? I *loved* the NHK collector, but what was the point of him? Merely a sense of threat? He led nowhere. So much not leading anywhere. Not sure if this is a whimsical Japanese characteristic, or just a weakness.

Biggest of all questions: why has nobody [that I know of] questioned the paedophilia aspects of the story? They're kinda glaring.

So I guess my final reaction is: *what the...?*

Anyway, the point is, the distraction's over with. Now I'm back to the real world and badgering away at things in order to build my own escape from and engagement with said. Making a story, making things with my hands, drawing all delicate-like, and painting. I feel like I've been relieved of a great burden.

Thursday, 22nd December, 2011.

Screwed

The good news is I got up as early as early and went for a walk even though I hadn't had enough sleep, because I'm trying to re-align my sleep patterns. The bad news is that when I go back to sleep after waking early, in order to make sure I get enough sleep if I happen to've gone for an early-as-early walk, say, I sometimes have bad dreams.

I think that this morning's bad dream was supposed to be erotic, but I woke up and laughed myself silly. Until I realised how tragic it was. I dreamt I was having sex with a vibrator, one that didn't have much kick. The tragic realisation in remembering this dream is that not only is the Man of My Dreams a mechanical device that requires batteries, but that even He's not a very good lover.

This doesn't bode well for my future; even my subconscious has given up.

Friday, 23rd December, 2011.

Tonight...

...when I came home from work, it was to the sound of my children playing the piano and laughing together. I stood in the garage for a while to listen, in case they stopped when I walked in. But they didn't stop. So nice.

First-Born, who didn't come to the family Xmas dinner last year, which made me so sad at the time, has gotten presents for everyone in the family and is looking forward to it this year. Also nice.

Tonight I got stabbed in the head by a hostile rose-ish bush when I was trying to murder it. Not so nice.

This heat, which you can't feel until you're out in it, has me invigorated and dripping with good, clean sweat when I'm down in the garden before sunset, grunting my way across our piece of hillside and climbing up and down the driveway, carting heavy branches and bundles of waste.

A good way to spend dusk, stabbing notwithstanding.

Monday, 26th December, 2011.

A Man's World

I entered one of these today. At least I think that's what it was. It did seem to have a lot of men in it.

I went swimming in a different area, to see what it's like Elsewhere. I knew it to be a heavily ethnic area so I was also kinda curious about who'd be swimming in that particular pool. Mostly I was hoping it'd be close to nobody, it being Boxing Day and stormy enough to guarantee a free lane all to myself. Almost. I shared with one man, who I happened to run over when I was doing back stroke because I didn't realise how fast I was swimming, but that's neither here nor there. Was beautiful water.

It was in the sauna afterwards that I realised how male the world is. There are men everywhere! I hadn't noticed just how many there are. You see them more clearly when they're all in together. And half naked. But that's also neither here nor there.

It was me and nine men at any given time. So crowded I couldn't lie down to relax, but that's okay. Just this once. It was the conversation I found interesting, because I don't often get to hear men just talking to each other. But not so interesting that I need to repeat what they said. The things Bike-Shorts Man was saying about his friend's housemate feeding all of the peanut butter to her fuck-buddy was almost interesting enough. Just not quite.

Because of the ethnic demographic and the way male community works in different ways Elsewhere, I wondered if I'd entered some sacred man space. I was comfortable, even though they all did a double-take when they saw me in there. Or maybe it has nothing to do with ethnicity; maybe women just don't use that sauna much. But I still think men are such foreign creatures (no pun intended). I have more male friends now than I've ever had, but that's not the same as eavesdropping on the sauna regulars. I learnt much.

Still Monday, 26th December, 2011.

Oh Yeah, That

I've been meaning to think aloud about Churchy Friend again, because she calls me a lot at the moment. The lead up to Xmas, despite me being a raving heathen.

Sometimes it's pointless trying to add to the conversation because I can't get a word in edgeways, so I just listen. And wonder why she calls me. She's completely forgotten that she doesn't even like me.

I haven't forgotten. So I listen, and when I do speak I don't like the sound of my voice. I don't like what I say to her. Maybe because it's getting-by conversation. She still doesn't ask me any questions so I don't get a chance to offer much. And when I do offer something it's hard to believe she gives much of a shit about anything I have to say. Why tell somebody a small part of a big story? She knows hardly anything about what I do inside my life and doesn't want to know.

So why, I wonder, does she still need me to be her friend? I can hear her not-liking me in her voice the same way I can hear my not-being-liked in mine. It's a pretty horrible thing for me to have to know.

It's nice that she jokes about us being in a nursing home together when we're old, so I guess that's it. I'm one of the few things she knows will be there all the way into her future, somebody she matters to. And we all need to matter to somebody. I think I matter to her, just not as much as she thinks I do. I wonder when she'll remember that again.

Tuesday, 27th December, 2011.

The Reason I Should Never Be Burgled

I don't have what a regular thief would want. No wide-screen tv, no up-to-date dvd player, no fancy-schmancy stereo system, no Wii and so on. No jewellery. No money stashed inside a mattress.

And yet... I have been burgled, albeit by a thief interested in the irregular. I went to see a movie with Mum and Ye Olde Sister today, and as I was walking Mum up the driveway I noticed that the yellow flowers I'd been gazing upon happily for a long time now had not disappeared due to witherment and death, but had actually been cut from my garden.

Stolen! They say it's disturbing to come home and find your undies drawer rifled through and your jewellery gone, but I think this is just as creepy. Somebody has eyed those beautiful flowers and then crept half-way down my driveway to steal them. They probably adorned somebody's Xmas dinner table. Motherfuckers.

The worst thing is that I can't get revenge or ever catch somebody at it. They're gone, and they'll stay gone until they grow again, and then I'll have to worry about them being stolen again.

That, dear people, is a stupid thing to have to worry about.

I loved them enough to photograph them. I sent the photo to Mum and I posted it in a conspicuous place so that everybody could see these unexpected happy things growing at my house. But now I hate loving things like flowers. Because look what happens when something's both beautiful and vulnerable to theft. Damn those flowers for suddenly appearing in my life. Damn the thief who took them from me. Damn everything to heck.

Wednesday, 28th December, 2011.

Perfect

As part of my Grand Plan I'm out to demonstrate that prefect happiness is the most boring thing ever. Not boring to me, because I'm too busy being happy to be bored. But boring to everybody else.

I love this week between Xmas and New Year's. The world has buggered off and there's no need to hurry anything.

The atmospherics of this perfection = today the sun is shining, literally but not too hotly, so I've thrown the windows open and can feel breezes, and the light's perfect and the house is clean and the children are quiet and the birds are singing (also literally), and time's standing still.

I've been lying around on my bed reading books I've already read and loved, the beauty of that being that I can love them again without needing to find out what happens. I already know what happens. This time I get to enjoy the happening for the sheer pleasure of it, and appreciate the writing as writing.

And I've been sitting at my desk, with my own writing open on my laptop, letting stories regain their momentum. And that's it, I'm in. The perfect quiet of it all. I'll be doing this every day, so that soon I'll having nothing interesting to say to anybody. Anything interesting that happens to me will be generated by my imagination and have no place in real-world conversation.

My conversations will start to look like this: *Hi Chris, how ya doing?/Hi, good/So what ya bin up to?/Oh you know, just writing/ Oh. Good/Yes, it is good/ Good. It's good to be good/Yes, yes it is.*

That's the best kind of boring ever. Never mind that in this grand plan I forget to ask people what they've been doing. That's because by the time I have these conversations I'll have crept so far into my stories I'll have forgotten how to be social. I only hope I'll have remembered to shower and brush my hair.

But anyway that's the near future and therefore forever away, because for now time really is standing still. There's a certain quality to it that I have to stop and acknowledge a hundred times a day. I'm not used to having peace like this again. The calm of my little family in this house. Happiness has crept back and stayed this time.

First-Born gave me money for groceries this morning, and when I said *'It's too much'* they said *'So? Because of all of the things you do'*.

Basically an acknowledgement of my doing. Not taking me for granted. Such a leap forward. This adds to the peace.

Yesterday, Son playing piano for his grandmother. Me feeding Mum bruschetta at my sunny big table before taking her to see a movie. *Good life*.

Friday, 30th December, 2011.

Party's Over

Whoa, dizzy. I didn't sleep a wink. It's not often you get to say that and mean it literally but really, I DID NOT SLEEP.

Giving up and going for an early morning walk made it worth it. I've missed the mornings. But it's time to acknowledge the insomnia, which was giving me a nudge and then got impatient, hence, being awake all night. That scares me because of my motor tic = what it does to my body if I don't sleep. It was starting to die down but I've noticed it increasing in momentum.

I have no idea why I have insomnia. I've been calm, not the least bit stressed or worried about anything, and I don't have a million thoughts racing through my mind when I go to bed. In fact, I lie there wondering why I'm so awake, but wondering quietly, a bit baffled.

This does provide me with an opportunity to panic. Because I keep thinking I have a whole two months left before I go back to Art School, and that seems like such a long time. But now I've realised that two months is only eight weeks. If I'd thought about it, that could have been sixteen weeks to work through, but I've fluffed about all calm and relaxed-like, making sure life's peaceful. Working on things, but only a little. And now half the holidays have gone.

When I've finished studying, every day will look like that perfect one, but for now = time has limits and I have to work like crazy between now and March. If the sound of time-running-out keeps me awake forever I won't be the least bit surprised.

Saturday, 31st December, 2011.

Mad Dogs n' Englishmen

I don't let myself go out into the sun these days because of the way I cook so easily, but (sorry for the repetition) I love the heat. So today I did, smack in the middle of the day. I went to the reservoir and I walked the whole park and it was beautiful. The sound of magpie larks, the smell of kangaroo poop baking in the sun, butterflies as big as birds.

The plan is that I wear myself out, so that I can sleep. Am still so very, very awake.

January 2012

Monday, 2nd January, 2012.

Just Thinkin'

I love how you can ring Readings on the phone and ask *'I was wondering if you have a particular book in stock'*, and the phone-answerer asks *'What book?'*, and you say *'Decameron'*, and instead of saying *'Decamwhat?'* he asks, *'Boccaccio?'*. This made me happy. Makes me think I'll one day meet these people who know who Boccaccio was and not be so book-lonely. One day one day.

For today, though, met Young Studio Peep at the Nova and saw *We Need to Talk About Kevin* for the second time. I loved it just as much as the first time. Either I'm really easily pleased or it's a brilliant movie.

But anyway, now I'm perfectly happy. And it's perfectly hot. When we stood outside on the footpath talking after the movie it was the perfect temperature. Like a sauna, but not. The air thick but not stifling. And there were so many thistledowny things blowing along the street outside of Readings, making the night seem surreal.

It's late. The insomnia's getting worse and worse, so instead of getting into bed where I'll be afraid of wakefulness, I'm going for a midnight walk with First-Born. And then [please, body o' mine], sleeeeeep.

Yesterday profoundly lonely, but today again released. Because nobody's expecting anything from me, so I have time to write and draw, and if that ever doesn't work out for me I can do other things.

It's hard starting. But once I'm in...

Just difficult knowing in advance that to do this, I have to embrace loneliness. And the emptiness of everything. Will connect soon. In the meantime = art.

Friday, 6th January, 2012.

One More for the Road

I'm re-listening to an audio reading of Markus Zusak's *The Book Thief*. I'm supposed to be avoiding darkness but there ya go, it's everywhere. And this is one of its most perfect expressions. So I was drawing away and forgot that the sad bit – which I knew was coming – would make me cry. I refused to put down the pencil when my eyes started to water. Made drawing very difficult.

But I did start wondering [again] why anybody would choose to be a writer. When most of what we write is dark in some way. That's the morose mood I'm in. I contacted a manuscript appraiser today to see if I should send a particular manuscript in, because I felt desperate to keep the wheels turning, mired as I am. And then I decided to send two. And then I felt guilty for spending so much money on a hope I can't even feel, because it's all actually so pointless.

I felt soiled writing the query emails, because I was putting myself into the world. Got to get over that. Because sometimes what I put into the world isn't bad. Is it?

This is the whole woe-is-me shebang, I think. I don't think I feel sorry for myself, but I'm wondering why the fuck I put myself through this crap instead of committing myself to an office job somewhere for five days a week and watching TV every easy night when I get home.

So on the eve of some intense re-working of fiction that I'm going to half-enjoy to the point of ecstasy and half-lament for the waste, all I can say is *here we go again...*

Saturday, 7th January, 2012.

Bird Slayer

Saving that which I had killed. The jesus bird. Magpie flew into the front of my car as I was driving. Slammed on brakes but not soon enough. Hit it hard. Cried. Life so ugly. Did u-turn. Went back for it. It was sitting upright in the gutter. Threw blanket over it and scooped it up. Sang to it as I drove. Took it to vet. It lived. Despite my singing. Things not so dark after all. Smiley face.

Monday, 9th January, 2012.

Roll Over Beethoven

I was going to go to bed early, but Son started playing the piano. This time First-Born and I were allowed to stand around and watch, even though he insists that I make him nervous.

Honest to goodness, it's euphoric to stand by when somebody plays the piano. He plays incredibly well, and bits of *Moonlight Sonata* are so, so beautiful. The feeling that must have pulsed inside Beethoven's mind when he composed the *dnt, dnt, dnt* bit. Wow. And the conversation between the three of us tonight. Laughing, even. How happy is it possible to be?

This is what I pictured our family life to be when my kids were young. These moments where you just enjoy things. Around a piano. How different is our home with my children playing music. And the clarity outside, the world I live in quite beautiful. Peace descending again.

Now First-Born's tinkering with the piano, and I'll wait 'til they've finished before sleeping. The *dnt dnt dnt* bit of *Moonlight Sonata* is resonating through my head so long after Son's finished playing it. I love it absolutely.

Wednesday, 11th January, 2012.

Deadline

It's funny how "deadline" has the word *dead* in it. I've become an expert at letting myself down, or at just not being what I used to be. I'm not so sad that I'm not functioning any more, but I still carry with me the realisation that there's not much point to anything.

I've been working on a drawing since November. Or a series of small drawings that work together. And I've had certain deadlines in my head all this time. I used to work to these deadlines, as incentive and because they present opportunities to be involved in something other than your own studio. I've never expected anything from them, they just added excitement to life. Gave measure to my days, or shape to the year.

I could easily have finished this drawing to meet the first deadline. But I didn't. I reasoned with myself but it was no use; I have no push left. What with there not being any point to anything at all.

Same with the writing. I work solidly, especially now, but I have no push. I don't know why I let a little bit of pointlessness get in my way, it never bothered me before. Except that it's not just pointlessness, it's a failure to believe in possibility. And yet, I'm so absorbed by this work it's confusing.

It's okay, though. Today, when I decided not to push for the deadline, I went up to the mailbox and pulled out an envelope that contained an entry form to another drawing thingy. What a wonderful bit of timing that was. Makes me laugh, it was so wonderfully timed.

Thank you, universe, for reminding me that there's no hurry. I'll do these things I need to do and I'll do them quietly. Because there's always a next time, and by then I'll be more ready.

Saturday, 14th January, 2012.

Catch Twenty-Two

We're all familiar with the catch 22 of publishing in contemporary Australia. You need publication success to prove your worth as a writer, but it's difficult to achieve publication success until you've proven your worth as such.

I've been in contact with some industry professionals recently because I'm such an up-sucker. No I'm not! I was joking! Really because I'm organising those manuscript appraisals. And a conversation I had with one particular professional today has put me off quite particularly.

One of the things she said was that publishers won't touch literary fiction. At all. Now I know it's difficult if that's what you write, but she made it sound so arbitrary I was taken aback. Because she did it in the context of offering other services.

It surprised me because of who she is, and because it was transparent that she's running a factory. A writing factory for the desperate. And that she's just a business woman. She was giving me a spiel, and wasn't smart enough – this very intelligent woman – to see that I was smart enough to see through it. I got the impression that she assumes everybody who rings her is after the same thing, and that she doesn't respect their individual circumstances much.

That's just dumb. Reducing everybody to some generic model of customer that'll rise to the sales pitch and fork out money.

I'm being cynical, but justifiably. A friend was telling me about a book she's been reading on the difference between social and market value, and it's given me a language to work with when considering the state of publishing now. Because when books are reduced to commodities, their social value's irrelevant beyond the scope of marketing potential. And the powers that be – or many of them, if you listen to discussions – seem to have lost the sense of discovery that allows them to feel wonderment at the possibility of something new.

Is that true? I don't even know for sure, but if it is, are *any* of them seeking the pleasure of discovery anymore? And if so, why do people allow an arbitrary approach to dominate the industry when it comes to submissions?

For now I'm remaining vigilant against the people who're trying to lure us into the commodity trap; not the publishers, but the many who offer related services. The ones who're cashing in on the desperate hoards (and there *are* hoards) by giving us a false sense of hope.

It's a stupid cycle and I won't be part of it. I can't be, because I'm not desperate. I'm too realistic. Used to be that authors were welcomed for what they can offer to the world. Now everybody's exhausted because of the glut, and authors are allegedly a pain in the arse. Like, not *another* one.

Just like in the studios, where the more elitist teachers aren't excited about a lot of art because they're too jaded by over-exposure. Almost the same. Maybe it is the same. Except, too many people love literature for it to be diminished like this. Surely?

Tuesday, 17th January, 2011.

And Today's Distractions Are... #1

A brother's daughter – my niece – is about to get married, and only one of his eight siblings have been invited to the wedding. That one sibling was not me.

She's the second born of a second born. This means nothing, but sounds very good, like it should be significant. If I ever make up a fable about them, that's how it'll start.

In my early twenties I was cut off from this niece – as I was from my other nieces and nephews – because I was in a relationship with a woman. I don't know how much of this I've written about before, but I'm thinking about it again now. The many cousins I thought my own children would grow up with were very sadly almost-absent from our lives.

It makes me bawl so I'm not letting myself think in too much detail, just enough to say that it was devastating. This wedding's making me remember things I'd rather forget.

―――

And Today's Distractions Are… #2

First-Born's gone away and didn't tell me. Again. So when they left at 5:30 this morning, after having woken me much earlier, I thought they were going for a walk and I couldn't sleep because I expected my sleep to be disturbed when they got back.

I got four hours' sleep. I've been getting four hours or less almost every night since just after Xmas. First inexplicably, and then because every time I settle in to a routine it gets broken by their nocturnal inconsistency.

And I wonder, why can't they just tell me what they're doing, so that I can plan around them? Why the secrecy? They've been much better lately, but things like this make me unhappy. Moreso because the manuscript re-working has me in such a state of remembering.

But anyway. Misery is crap and the solution to everything is: forget everything else, and write a book.

―――

Wednesday, 18th January, 2012.

Cryptography

Just quietly, *I've broken the code*. That's how it feels. This manuscript, years old, always *this close* to publishing according to everybody but publishers; it had a re-writing code to break and I think I've done it.

It's been declared too confronting by publishers, mostly. So I've softened it with every re-working. The voice = you can't sustain that voice for a long novel because the reader will tire of it. I've known this but haven't known how to crop the thing. Because all of its bits are necessary. Allegedly. Or so I've been told.

But this week I realised I could courageously remove a whole narrative thread. In fact, I started to hate this thread. And now it seems so much cleaner. Because there was too much emphasis on sex and sensuality as an expression of the need for emotional connection. The problem being that the idea of sex dominates so much that the reader can't see the emotion any more.

I didn't see this before because I was in my thirties when I wrote it. Now that I'm in my forties I'm just so much more wise [hah]. And perhaps bored by the idea of sexuality being an expression of the need for emotional connection.

The other thing I did was alter patterns of speech that characterised the voice as contemporary. This voice was supposed to be powerful and new. If it becomes less new the more you're exposed to it, then it loses its power. I think I might have altered it enough this time around to have kept the voice fresh without a sense of dragging? Again, cleaner. Something I couldn't manage before, something I couldn't see.

I'm rattling on as though this would mean anything to anybody but myself, but it feels to have butchered a manuscript so violently that it now looks like something else entirely.

This is why I love writing. Because every time you engage with your work a process of metamorphosis takes place. You can't share the insides of that process with many people, but it's a very exciting thing.

Thursday, 19th January, 2012.

Planet Rich People

When I say that Friend With Rich Parents has rich parents, I mean only that her parents own more than one property, and that some of the property they own is on an exotic island somewhere, and that they own a house boat and a speed boat, and run a business, and the wife doesn't work, and they travel a lot and so on and so on. To put it into perspective, their main home is on the foothills around the corner from mine, on the fringe of outer suburbia. So the richness could be relative for all I know – they could be to Rich what soft porn is to Pornography. Poor-Man's Rich.

The relevance is that Friend With Rich Parents is, like me, a single parent. The difference between us is that she gets a company car without having a job. She doesn't have to work, or pay for her own petrol. Her parents take her on all-expenses-paid holidays. She doesn't have to pay rent because she lives in a house owned by her parents. When she starts sending her children to private secondary school, her parents will pay for it. And so on and so on.

Last night I was looking out the windows, as I do, at the view. Very green, evening light all thick, air full of birdsong et cetera. Lonely, but nice. And as it started to grow dark I took my lonely self out for a walk. As I was passing Friend With Rich Parents' Parents' house, I heard a car and my name being called, and turned around to find an emergency light glaring from their car roof (BMW convertible), and drunken festivity beckoning me over.

One of many things I love about these people (apart from them being genuinely nice) is that I hardly ever see them, hardly even know them, but they treat me like family. They're always so genuinely friendly and happy to see me, and will accost me for conversation for great stretches of time on the roadside outside their house. I like that. I like that even though I'm lonely for something more substantial, I have pockets of people that settle like a blanket of community around me.

So anyway. Friend With Rich Parents was with them last night. I haven't seen her for years. Haven't wanted to, because we live on different planets. We talk every now and then on the phone, and did so a few nights ago. So hey, what a coincidence. I said to her then if she's at her parents' house she should join me for my walk, which she's done before. So she did.

We went inside to talk with her parents first, and they're very warm. They kept asking me to stay for drinks and hugging me and kissing my cheek, talking to me like excited kids, each of them speaking over the other to be at the centre of the conversation. The friendliness,

I told you – it has me baffled, but I love how nice they are. And how social. Then her mum kept hugging me and saying *'I'm so proud of you'*, to which I asked *'Proud? Why?'* (thinking as I was about how I'm not quite anything in the world at the moment), and she said that I've grown into *'such a beautiful young woman'* and that I *'walk with such confidence'*.

I think it's because she mostly sees me in the dark, but I'll run with it. It was very sweet. I did correct her by telling her that it's too late for *'young woman'*, that I'm now borderline *'old bag'*. But that's okay. I do walk with something like confidence, even if it's only physical and kinda accidental, because I'm fit and love walking.

So, the walk. I'm a bit mean because I suggested to Friend With Rich Parents that we do the big walk. That's because I wanted more time for conversation, even though we really do live on different planets. One look at her, though, and I knew she'd find it difficult. Not fit, let's say. She was knackered before we got half way, and had pulled a muscle. Just by walking! It amazes me how people don't walk. As though they'd be happy if we could insert motorised wheels in our feet.

Meanwhile, my muscles were in heaven, working those hills. I love the stretch. Apparently I love it selfishly.

I feel sad for her. Not just because she was telling me about her sputum test. (Yes, really.) Anybody who talks about having a sputum test (unless they're actually very seriously ill) has to be felt sorry for. But because she was telling me about the self-help books she reads. Something about cocooning, and how they made her realise she needs to look after herself and her needs. So this is her cocooning year. Also she told me about the courses she does, all of them self-help. Neighbourhood house jobs. And the groups she's part of. Why I feel sad for her is that it's all so hippy and self-absorbed and boring. She spends all of her energy on managing her life rather than living it. She doesn't actually *do* anything.

I love her, but I can't relate to that. At all. So the best part of the walk for me was when we were about twenty minutes from home and walking up another hill and she told me a story about a turtle. A real story – one with a point. It was beautiful. It was what I've been working with lately in my writing, and I'm going to steal it and change it to give it meaning. I'll tell her and credit her experience, of course. I'm not really stealing it; I'm making something out of it. It's just the clay. But this is what I'm thriving on at the moment, little stories and modes of storytelling. I couldn't tell her about it, I can hardly tell anybody. All I can do is keep writing and hope they get to see it one day.

I AM SO EXCITED BY STORIES, is the point.

She was exhausted by the time I delivered her back to her parents' house. I wasn't. I'd walked a lot slower than usual and hadn't even broken a sweat. It's made me realise how strong my body is. And now I'm home and not really tired. I'm scared of going to bed, because if I can't feel sleepy I'll lie there, awake. So I'll just turn that turtle story over and let it grow fat on my own additions, I guess. Sigh.

Friday, 20th January, 2012.

The problem with America

A lot of people will have already said this, no doubt, but the problem with America is that it's so American.

By that I mean insular. I was just reading about the background of the movie *We Bought a Zoo,* and discovered that it's based on the experiences of Benjamin Mee. An English guy, autobiographical author. As in, from *England*. Which means that the Rosemoor wildlife park in the movie is not so much based on the Dartmoor zoo, but is a bastardisation thereof.

With a story like this, based in an English speaking country with a culture similar enough to their own, why did they feel the need to change the setting to California? Especially to California, which automatically adds an element of cheap [tacky] to any storyline.

Are American audiences really so self-absorbed that they can't summon enough interest in seeing a movie with a story based outside their own country? Do they need to hijack all stories into their own culture so that they own them, the same way that the dirty xtians did during the medieval period, when they sent their missionaries out to absorb local lores to add muscle and a false history to the xtian story?

Seriously America, wake yourself up and let the world be the world, and not just some subsidiary of your own country.

p.s. Just like American publishers not allowing australianisms or their equivalent in non-American-authored novels, putting them through a process of american-ification, but that's another subject altogether. Point being, American audiences aren't allowed to be curious; it really is the home of rampant homogeneity. A bit appalling, yah.

---

p.p.s.
When Prodigal Friend was at my house recently we took the babies out for a walk in the pram at night (the hazard of visiting me – you get dragged out on walks) and as we walked around a particular part of the hillside I could hear the most gentle little bird whistles up in the tops of the trees. It's a very sweet sound, tiny whistles in multitudes, and I told Her Son that it was made by the snoring birds.

For a long time I've puzzled over these snoring birds. Every time I walk under them, if I'm out at night. I visualise their little beaks and the whistles leaking through their little beak nostrils. Wondering how a species doesn't make itself vulnerable by being so noisy that a predator could find them really easily.

Then last night, Friend With Rich Parents corrected my illusion: she told me that they're not snoring birds, they're frogs.

With such a soft sound! Now I have to see the whole night landscape differently. I have to re-orient my senses from tree top to ground level. I have to re-visualise. It's weird how attached we get to our perceptions.

Hah. Frogs. Who'da thought? I don't know how I'm gonna break the news to Prodigal Friend's son.

Monday, 23rd January, 2012.

YTT
Watching the new *Young Talent Time* was kinda beautiful. I don't mind admitting that I looked forward to it, and that I dreaded it at the same time because I thought contemporary performers would fuck it up, by being all contemporary. But they didn't; it was sweet and innocent like it used to be, was all about really beautiful singing, interesting musical

interpretation, and if I describe those kids as being hyped up on red cordial I mean it in the nicest possible way. They're amazing.

Well done, people.

So as my kids walked through the kitchen area behind me and looked at the screen and said *'What the fuck?'*, I sat there remembering being in my pyjamas and ready for bed on a Saturday night when I was a kid, watching *Young Talent Time*. I'd told Churchy it was on, and she being of the same sentimental ilk we sent as many texts between us as it would take to have a conversation throughout the whole thing.

We can do that because I'm not so hard-nosed that I can ever reject her. But she sent a text saying she should come here and watch it with me on Sunday night. I'm supposed to be going out on Sunday night, but I don't wanna do either thing. The latter because I'm not feeling very social, the former because Churchy Friend keeps saying *let's do this* and *let's do that* as though she's completely forgotten how little she likes me. She's trying very hard to establish the kind of friendship we had before she snapped it in half.

Not sure what to make of her and I'd rather not have to deal with it. I can't look forward to seeing her. I don't trust her. And that's sad, because the memory of being in our pyjamas watching *Young Talent Time* when she visited our house when we were little is a nice one.

Anyway who am I trying to kid? Nice memories are sad. One of the texts I sent said something about how each of the team were very open about how much they love their families, and I finished it with *'my kids suck'*. Because they lost that love somewhere along the way. And with it they lost the energy for good stuff that these hyped up red cordial kids still have. It's like I can't enjoy anything anymore without experiencing that loss. Fucken fucken fuck.

Tuesday, 24th January, 2012.

It Speaks!

Son came out of his bedroom tonight. I went into that dark animal den to ask him about a download and this teenage boy who doesn't like being around me much at the moment (all of us in the house all of the time, he just needs his space, very normal) started a conversation. At first it was about downloads, him teaching me more about what to look for (a bit like reading a storybook to a five year-old; I had to keep reminding him that I'm not completely computer illiterate), and then onto other things.

We do have these conversations every now and then, it's just that it's been a while since the last one. This time he asked me what I actually do, as in what I studied before and what I'm studying now. Forgive me if I find these questions hilarious [!!!] but anyway, I managed to fill in the gaps of things that were vague to him, and we talked about the nature of contemporary art and writing things that we sometimes do talk about and so on...

...and then he asked me why on earth I've chosen to do two insanely intensive things (writing and art) instead of doing something rational to balance out the crazy of one or the other. For example, he's going to write, but he's also going to do IT because he loves it. He could do Physics because he loves it but that's another crazy and he doesn't want two crazies. He's much more sensible than me.

I loved this conversation. It was priceless. And he was saying what I've been saying to myself lately: pick one thing, do one thing, take the pressure off. Beautiful. I wish it were that simple. But he's inspired me to follow through on my Do One Thing goal. Because LIFE WOULD BE SO EASY if I just did ONE THING.

At the moment I think that thing is drawing; the art thing I started doing before I did Other Art. Full circle. The thing that makes me so calm and happy. (As I write this my mind goes off on tangents, so *that* drawing includes normal drawing and expressive drawing and animation and the sewy-fabricky printmaking installation things I want to do... I have to tell myself STOP IT!) (And what about clay? How can I give up clay?) (Seriously, stop it!)

But anyway. We got onto the nature of narrative in games versus novels, a very long discussion hindered by his inexperience with literary fiction and my inexperience with more complex games, but a great conversation nonetheless. Then he showed me a game called...? Oh fuck, I've forgotten. An indie game – he played it, I watched, and it was beautiful. But not overtly narrative.

Now my head's full of new stuff. What a nice night. Worth staying up 'til forever o'clock for this. I love my kids.

Note from the future: the game was Limbo.

After an indulgent bit of gluttony, I got *Homeland* out the way. Good tv, was very distracting. But now I've had my feed, and am sated.

Wednesday, 25th January, 2012.

Days is Long, Ain't They?

I have a craving for sourdough bread that I can't satisfy because we're out of sourdough bread. Sometimes I hate the contents of my fridge.

Today I watched *Super 8* and found it to be a less attractive version of *ET*.

Today I also watched *Jane Eyre* and found it to be very good at being *Jane Eyre*. Though I have to say I would prefer *Jane Eyre* if it had fucking in it.

Today I also worked at gathering the contents of a short story, but I did not write said short story.

Obviously I can't concentrate to save meself.

Still Wednesday.

Psycho Chicken [Allegedly]

Of course I'm not a psycho chicken, I can state that categorically. So before I tell you about the psychological profile I just read I have to fill in some background.

I was stupidly happy before Xmas (screaming it from the mountain tops), because First-Born had been friendly to me for a great length of time. Comparatively. It was also because of many other things, but that was a majority factor.

Then during Prodigal Friend's stay First-Born and I snuck out for a midnight walk, and they were in a foul mood that night so instead of our respectful silence (each using our own iPods), they started up a conversation. First-Born's walk conversations are antagonistic, hence the iPods. Best to avoid talking.

When we returned from what was a very stressful walk, we stayed at the top of the driveway for over an hour talking more, because First-Born chose that moment to tell me what was wrong with me. They said the only reason they were able to be nice to me lately was because they'd diagnosed me [via the internet] with a particular psychological disorder. They said that every time they feel angry at me they remind themself that I can't help being revolting because I have this very serious condition that makes it impossible for me to be nice.

I laughed, of course. In an incredulous way. Of all of the disorders they could've tried to pin on me, how on earth did they choose that one? I hadn't read the disorder profile, but the name's a dead give-away for a condition that there's no way in hell I could possibly have.

I laughed and let them speak. They can think what they like, if it means they'll be friendly to me. Even though it stings that their opinion, even when they're being nice, is a thing of cruelty that they can't resist inflicting. The last thing they're going to let me feel is loved.

Anyway, tonight I made the mistake of looking at the afore-unmentioned profile, to see what exactly it is First-Born thinks I am. Because they stopped being nice to me a short while ago. Three weeks?

It's sinking in again that things may never improve. Unless I get a lobotomy and just forget everything.

―――

Woken early, another talk with First-Born, started off antagonistic but then just emotional and then both talking solutions and about what we want from family. Lovely child, I knew it. So relieved, and happy, and optimistic again.

―――

Thursday, 26th January, 2012

Epiphany

A moment in which I realise [again] that writing's an awful thing to do. Ya know how sometimes you read fiction and think '*This is stupid, it isn't even real'*, and at other times – most times – you're completely swept away? But always there's this knowledge: when you draw or paint, you look up after your day's work and you've made a thing. The making of things is good. Not just things, but things that are [sometimes] worth loving. And I realise that I'm in a position to make these things ALL THE TIME. A sense of satisfaction at the end of each day. A sense of doing.

When you write, after a day's work all you have is a few pages of words that might take years to add up to a book that'll take years of labour and cause a lot of heartbreak before it even gets published IF EVER, and is therefore not likely to ever become a *thing*.

So I should try *not* to be a writer. I don't know how to not-be a writer. It's one thing to not-write – I can go for great lengths of time without actually writing. But it's another thing entirely to deliberately not-write. And to stop the thinking that compels the writing.

This could be what I want. So, a decision. For a short while I'll allow myself to write in the mornings, as though it's a job I have to do, but my bigger commitment will be to make art every day. I can do that because I love making art. So no matter how much time I waste on the telling of stories, I'll at least have things to show for my labour. And then one day, maybe I can shake the writing altogether. When the dismal reality of how crappy it is *really* sinks in. Then I'll be closer to doing my just ONE THING. Is it possible?

Friday, 27th January, 2012.

The Thing Won't Die

Well I thought that was a great bit of resolve, but then I went for a walk and the novel I'd just successfully killed in my mind started happening in my... *other* mind. The storyline. Over and over and over. More than that; the essence of it. I've unfortunately been listening to a certain bit of movie score that fits my narrative perfectly, and with music comes pathos. Over and over and over, all of the feelings but none of the words. Or not the ones I need.

I have to write the thing, but the writing's still as impossible as ever. Still too many projects. The ones I told myself I could drop, I kept as little things on the side. Little brain affairs, if you like, to indulge when the other projects aren't looking. As though they wouldn't take up time or headspace. Am I really that stupid?

Fuck. Back to square one in terms of planning. I have to treat my art projects like a novel, each one a chapter that I can map out and work on as an independent thing, even though it's part of a whole.

How the hell am I going to focus? All of these hours. They'll *run out*.

Monday, 30th January, 2012.

Ghost of Projects Past

Okay this is getting ridiculous and I need to empty my mind asap, a bit like evacuating a bowel. A mental enema.

For days and days now when I sit down to write, scenes roll through my mind. A memory of painting attached to a kind of longing for that. A memory of drawing. And the memory of an animation I haven't even started working on yet. Sometimes the making of things with clay. So that while I'm trying to determine my plot properly and get to the smoother part of the writing, my mind's operating on a hundred different levels, all at once. Thinking thinking thinking. The thinking that precedes projects, plotting, planning.

And when it's not scenes of doing, it's bits of writing, arrangements of words, struggles with plot, not for my novel but for other things. I can't commit to one thing. And I know it's because I haven't allotted times to the other projects – if I give them their time they wouldn't have to hover at the edge of my mind and step in to ask me very politely to give them some attention whenever I settle in to do something else. They'd be satisfied, knowing that I'll get to them when their next allotted time comes around.

The novel won't happen smoothly until I get all of it right, and fall into a healthy routine. I KNOW THIS but I can't seem to DO IT.

So before I settle in to work today I need to organise shit. And before I do that I have to think a few thoughts, starting with Strawberry Picking.

Strawberry Picking

This activity will now also be known as Dirt Harvesting, the two things inextricably linked. Because I needed red soil, and thought I'd have to go to the middle of Australia to get it. Or at least up as far as Mildura. Who has time to go to Mildura? One of my art projects would be less wonderful without it. I was craving red dirt more than I crave chocolate.

But then as I was planning the day of strawberry picking with Mum I remembered, clear as day, that we pick strawberries from red earth. I got so excited. Filled my car with bags and a shovel and gloves. Waited for Little Sister to arrive, told her about my sinister ulterior motive for the day, and off we went to meet up with our mother.

I was so obsessed with the idea of this dirt, I forgot that it's been a while since I've left a) my house and b) the city. So I got that shock I always get when I end up somewhere peaceful, and beautiful, and I was so energised by the idea of dirt-theft and beauty that I ended up having the best morning since forever.

Truth is, before yesterday I didn't want to go strawberry picking. I went to please my mother. I've been so wrapt up in project-thinking that I haven't wanted to see anybody. I've missed out on two social events that I wanted to go to. I hated the idea of Little Sister spending the whole day with me and then coming back here for the night. I couldn't stand the idea of not working on anything for *an entire day*. And I couldn't even imagine ever feeling really happy, because of the self-inflicted loneliness.

But then I was happy. So happy. Because being a shut-in is VERY BAD FOR YOU. I need people, and to be out driving through nice places in the [glorious!] heat in search of strawberries and dirt. These things are essential for good living.

So anyway, I had no idea just how red that soil would be. Mother was late so I pulled over and respectfully took what I needed from the planet. Little Sister shook her head and watched for oncoming traffic. With shovel in hand and furtive actions I felt like I was about to get rid of a body or something. I suspect it's illegal to take dirt from any old where, so let's just say I didn't dig away at a roadside in the morning shade to get my dirt. I didn't stop digging and throw my shovel down every time a car went by. Didn't stoop to fill the bags and hide them in the boot of my car. Anyway what dirt? I don't see any dirt. It was somebody else, I swear officer. They went thataway.

Needless to say, now I wish I could go strawberry picking every day. It was so nice being out with my people. A good reminder of how I need life to be happy, not just stories. And strawberries, eaten fresh from the stalk in the middle of a sun-baked field.

Little Sister

That was the first time I've given her a day for a long, long time. Given her any time, actually. She's been asking and I haven't been giving.

But yesterday, so generous. Starting off with the strawberries, where I thought it might not end well because she got impatient with Mum having to stop her car to give the kids (Niece and Nephew) drinks. Little Sister never had kids and isn't entirely tolerant of what it takes to manage life with them in tow.

I was more than ready to be annoyed at her for being like that. Also annoyed when she got impatient with me about the second dirt harvest, after the strawberry picking, saying *'Well if we do that then we should skip the picnic because we haven't got time'*. I was thinking *fuck you* at her in my mind. Not because I'm a bogan, but because I didn't want to have to drive so far to get it later when I was already there. And because time for what? She was coming back to my house, we didn't have a time limit on that. We had all the time in the world.

I'll have to tell her that just now I realised she's like Dad. For example, when we drove to Broken Hill he was great, exploring the world just like I was and loving every inch of it. But on the way home he wouldn't stop. I wanted to get fresh oranges in Mildura (orange capital of the world!) for myself and for Mum, who would've been tickled pink, but he said no because you can buy oranges in the shops and we didn't have time. *Of course* we had time. Neither of them make sense like that.

So I got more dirt, and we had our picnic, and the day was wonderful. She became patient and all was well.

During the afternoon she took me to get the iPhone I've been trying to talk myself out of getting. I have no idea why she was impatient being out in the nice place and not the least bit impatient being in a shopping centre, but anyway. Got the thing.

And then at home she asked to see my art work. I didn't she hadn't seen my paintings; years' worth of paintings. I dragged them out from the racks I'd built and with her I saw them like I was seeing them for the first time. Not the ones I hate, but the ones I felt (really really felt) when I was working on them. So all of my plans to just do One Thing have gone entirely out the window, and all of the little painting daydreams that've been playing over and over in my mind when I'm trying to write have turned back into enormous painting daydreams.

I can't even begin to describe that feeling, but it's there, and it's urgent. Urgent-ish. Hence I'm sitting here coughing it up instead of working on my novel.

And just like that, the probability of spending time with little sisters n' such just shrunk. Enter the never-ending [and ugly] irony, of quality time spent with other people reminding you that you don't have time to spend quality time with other people. Too much to do! You can spend quality time with people when you've finished these too many things! Whenever that is.

---

i-me

Ah, the iPhone. I've gone and done it. For a few reasons, but it's costing me twice as much as my regular plan so I still feel squeamish.

When I first thought about getting one I asked Son what he thought and he said *'No, don't do it'*, because giving me an iPhone would be like *'giving a television to a monkey'*. That is, a monkey will like the lights and whistles, but it won't ever be able to fully appreciate what a television can do.

He's not calling me stupid, exactly, but he is kinda calling me technologically challenged. And he was passionate about it, as though I was insulting the technology by even thinking about it. As though me having an iPhone would be a certain kind of sacrilege, because I could never love it as fully as it needs to be loved.

Little Sister, yesterday, who really was good company, and who managed somehow to keep Son interested for quite a long time – as in, he came out of his room and stayed there talking with us for hours – has an iPhone. I'm swearing now that I won't ever use it the way I see other people use it. Because Son's right. I'm not interested in apps or games or gimmicks. Siri isn't turned on. And watching Little Sister with hers all day, I was reminded of how socially disturbing they are. She plays *Words with Friends* with Baby Bogan Brother and his wife, so all day I only had half of her attention. Her conversations were held with her head down over that thing.

It's not in my character to be like that. Just so you know. I haven't joined the other side. i-swear.

Brain-Dump:
Complete.

February 2012

Wednesday, 1st February, 2012.

Hip Hip Hip...
Today I'm stealing Prodigal Friend's birthday for my re-birthing, because the first day of every month comes with its own drum roll. Luckily I don't have to squeeze myself through a vagina to be reborn, although it will require a shift of cranial plates to get through the process.

I let myself achieve monumental failure yesterday in preparation for this big event. I'm enjoying the failure because it gives me time to read and reading's making me happy. I'm surprised my eyes aren't aching yet.

So, today. From now on I will do Everything I plan to do. I won't be torn between projects because I'll be giving time to all of them.

So far so good. So far. Good.

Tuesday, 7th February, 2012.

Conditions Apply
It's not always inspired writing, but any writing is good writing and it's happening every day so I guess I can safely say *'I'm in'*.

I've abandoned the idea of Doing One Thing; it's more realistic for me to aim for Doing One Thing at a Time. And jumping back into the whirlwind of exhibition launches and dinners and drinks and taiko and lunches and galleries with all of my lovely friends has reminded me I'm very lucky to have these people.

The horrorscope writer for Saturday's paper (*The Age*) has gone back to writing stuff I can look forward to every week even-though-i-don't-believe-in-it, instead of that literary bullshit (full of Piscespoet-Auden quotes and so on) that was dished out over summer. An example, to validate my new approach to the doing of Everything:

> With Neptune, your sponsor planet, moving into Pisces for the foreseeable future, your special assets and talents come into their own. As usual, conditions apply: which are that you ground yourself with sound practises, get feedback from people you respect and reassess how you allocate your energy.

The horrors have spoken, and I couldn'ta said it better meself.

Wednesday, 8th February, 2012.

Spick n' Span

That's what my novel has to be. No literary pollutants soiling the thing. Which is why it's so hard to write. I have to keep reminding myself that a genre piece is a clean piece, and you have to find other ways to make it beautiful, without clogging up the pipes and interrupting the flow.

Also I'm timid because even though I went all the way to Japan to experience the place first hand, writing about the unfamiliar is still scary. This is exactly the way I felt when I was writing historical (medieval) fiction, and I had to push myself through it. But I found a way to make that beautiful; all I had to do was wait for the poetry to hit me, or the feeling for words you get when a place becomes rich and alive for you. To get there I have to push and push, be bland even though I'm screaming inside, until suddenly I've built enough of that world for me to stop and look around more closely. Then I'll feel it.

It'll happen. Just reminding myself to own it. The story's mine, all I have to do is tell it. Therein lies the hard work.

Friday, 17th February, 2012.

Exhilaration!

I have to pause to express this before I take myself off to the drawing table. Because what a buzz, and what a great way to live, with your head always wrapped up in a story that you're inventing as you go. When you're reading or watching a movie you only get what they give you, and you spend it quickly because you're hungry and greedy, and you want more but you can't have it so you have to thrive off-of the resonance and it fades painfully until there's not enough left and you have to go hunting for more. But when you're writing it, you get to live inside it and touch all of its fibres, strand by strand.

Bliss!

I've been writing the thing in an almost skeletal draft form, letting fragments of real writing with real flesh on them slip in when they appear in my mind, but for the most part keeping the momentum up so that I'm walking myself through the action. The plan is to get to know my characters and the story so well that when I go back in for the next draft I can relax into the nature/shape/flavour of the storytelling with a Real Voice, because I'll have faith in where it's going. I get to colour in the outline, in other words.

Both parts of this process are incredibly fun for different reasons. When it's not killing me, it's complete and utter joy. This is the feeling I want to remember; elaborate, intense and exciting.

It's exciting because I'm no longer afraid of the Japan bits, or the unfamiliarity of the geography or customs. I'm so immersed in the landscape I've created it'll be hard to go back to the Australian bits when I have to.

I'm so immersed, in fact, that for the last two days – having been stuck on a particular part of the story and therefore spending that time drawing instead – I found it really hard not to write. The reward is that today, because of that mental break, and because it enabled me to get my drawing to an advanced enough state that I don't have to panic [much] about getting it finished on time, I was able to very easily sit at my computer and write that difficult chapter, and then some. All of the bits falling into place. Writing skeletal is the best approach ever.

So there ya go. When I write these days I'm hammering at the keys with the same speed and urgency I use when writing a blog entry, where I can be fast and just think at speed because I'm not focused on the craft of writing, I'm just letting it all fall out (as you can see by the sloppiness of these paragraphs). I love that sound. So much writing time is spent in silence that when those keys get a marathon work-out you really feel like you're doing something. Probably because you are.

Tuesday, 21st February, 2012.

Ancient Skilles

I've wanted to learn how to paint fresco since I can remember, so when I found out I could do just that I nearly tripped over myself to get to it. How lucky, to have access to somebody able to pass on skills that belong to sometime else. And it's every bit as exciting as I thought it'd be. Difficult, yes, but in an ace way. I could EAT the stuff.

At first I had to copy an old artist, something I've always said I'd never, ever do. It was more fun than I expected it to be. Except, I had thoughts as I was doing it. Such as, you labour to represent the original work as faithfully as possible, but at the same time are aware that some of the original artist's marks were made much more casually, and that makes it silly to copy because if you were really copying you'd be making your own casual marks instead of being so accurate. If that makes sense. Della Francesca will be half turning in his grave, and half looking back over his ghostly shoulder to say 'Not bad... for a first try'.

What a whirlwind couple of days. The teacher was wonderful, even though she's the second person I've come across in a single week who happens to be the almost-spitting image of Ex-Girlfriend-Not-Girlfriend. It's very hard to actually see somebody who seems so much like somebody else; you have to keep making an effort to believe that this person isn't really that person pretending to be the other person. And it's hard to stand back and let this person's personality be different from her almost-double.

Anyways, a nice way to return to painting. I feel transformed, and can't wait to take the medium and run with it. I have to be careful with how I use it, because imagine walking into the studios at school and telling them I've learnt something so old-fashioned. There'd be heart-attacks and looks of horror. It's best not to tell them. Show them instead, but wait until I've used it my way. Which hopefully isn't going to seem too old-fashioned for them, because being ancient and doing ancient is a dangerous combination in that place. (43 years old!)

Anonymosity

Not that I care. I've added a new thing to my list of Things I Have to Do, and it fits beautifully into everything else. As long as I love it, it doesn't matter. If that ain't strength of character I don't know what is.

(Delusional? Probably, but let's just focus on the bliss.)

March 2012

Sunday, 4th March, 2012.

Love Silences

Another year, another birthday, another opportunity for my children to say *'Happy Birthday'* to my face, hug optional. But they didn't. Again. First they forgot my birthday, then when I reminded them they each said *'What? Is that the date? Holy shit!'* and some such. But neither followed their holy-shit with a *'Happy Birthday'*. I know this because I waited for it.

Love Languages

I don't read yer average popular philosophy or motivational kinda book, but every now n' then somebody tells me about one that sounds like it has a bit of merit. I remember years ago Churchy Friend telling me about some churchy guy who wrote about the languages of love, plural, and it made sense. We each read love a certain way, responding to particular gestures. For some people the sign of love is gift-giving; for some it's verbal, for some tactile, for some demonstrated through acts of kindness (or was it service?), et cetera. Clearly my children don't speak verbal love. I wish I could work out their language so that I wouldn't feel sad when they fail to wish me a happy birthday.

However #One

I was cooking bolognese last night and said to Son that parents who have kids who want to be chefs are lucky. He asked why and I said because their kids do the cooking. Then I asked *'Ever thought about being a chef, Son?'*, to which he answered *'Well you're probably luckier because I'm going to work in IT and that means I'll probably have a lot of money and you'll benefit from that'*.

Hopefully I won't *need* to benefit from that, but it was kinda sweet. I suspect his Love Language is an *'I'll look after you'* one.

However #Two
First-Born's been getting better and better. The rudeness has gone, almost completely. When it's there I'm able to address it. We have rational discussions. We have *conversations*. We walk together. And laugh. Then last night, when I was dropping them at the station, before they got out of the car they leant over to give me a kiss. They're very soft, my first born. And as I drove off I started crying. Because it wasn't a spontaneous spur of the moment kiss that would be followed by horribleness in the near future; it was a kiss that arose from the gradual getting-betterness of our relationship.

However #Three
Son plays the piano beautifully, I've mentioned that already. But he won't play it in front of me. If I'm lucky he'll be playing when I get home from a walk and I'll be able to hide outside and listen. And I am [lucky] and I do [spy].

I heard him playing last week and was blown away first by how beautiful the piece was, and second by how he'd managed to learn a whole new long and difficult score without my knowing it in a very small space of time.

Son: *Were you standing outside listening?*

Me: *No, no Son, I just happened to have heard you as I got home...*

He reminded me that he doesn't like playing in front of me because I'm a people, although he doesn't mind playing when First-Born's home because he doesn't consider First-Born a people.

BUT... on Thursday, I was home and working downstairs when he moved to the piano and started playing that very beautiful piece, so I got to listen to it good n' proper. I cried then, too. Rapture and euphoria – the spontaneous playing of music does that to me. And because my theory is that he did it on purpose so I could listen, as a kind of gift. Maybe because he forgot my birthday and didn't wish me a happy one.

Swimming

I love it. I wish I could write odes to swimming and serenade beneath its window. It's one of the things I love most at the moment, being in the water, where it's silky and peaceful. I wish I had my own lap pool and sauna so that I could do this every day. Without running into other people's Band-Aids.

I've found a quiet pool that's too far away, but I go there because it's so nice. I'm going to go there now, hoping the rain has kept other swimmers (and their Band-Aids) away. I can finish my think later.

Oh swimming, how do I love thee....

Monday, 5th March, 2012.

The Dream

I'd hate for my brain to be predictable, but really, I can trace this one back to many places. Starting with Arty Taiko Friend talking to me about working on her relationship with her husband, and asking me about whether or not I'd work on my relationship with my ex-husband. Me explaining to her that the way he rejected my child is irredeemable behaviour, and then some.

Actually I explained it more complicatedly than that, but still. Couple that with First-Born being very First-Bornly lately and letting their guard down, and the signs of Bad Times Ending, and my dream makes a lot of sense.

Dream Ex-Husband was apologising to First-Born for all of his awful intolerance. He apologised to First-Born and then explained to me in great depth that he could see what he'd done wrong. And I hugged him with real affection because it was a very big leap of understanding.

I woke up disappointed, because it wasn't real. He's still the intolerant person he was, he still refuses to understand the more complex emotions that drive people – particularly children – and he'll therefore most likely be alone forever. We're still friends and I really don't want him to be alone. I guess I feel disappointed all over again that he hurt my child so deeply, and that he rejected the vibrant life we gave him because of the hard emotional work involved. And that he never understood exactly what that meant.

In some ways I'd like to love him again, but I never will. Not romantically, and not with trust. Because he's a lovely person, but he can't undo what I've witnessed. And anyway he's past the point of tolerance with us. Our us-ness shits him up the wall if he's exposed to us for too long.

Stupid dream. I still want to protect First-Born from that rejection. Maybe also to protect myself.

Wednesday, 14th March, 2012.

The Baffling Inner Workings of...

...my mind. Please forgive, but another dream happened, a doozy, and I can't stop thinking about it.

For some reason I was unhappy with my height. My height was intolerable and I was having surgery to shorten myself by a couple of inches, by cutting inches away from my spine. That was dark psyche, and my parents were there all serious-like to support me.

Before they performed this macabre cosmetic surgery, the team had to remove my skin. *All* of it. And I was awake while they peeled it from my body. I remember looking down at the softness being tugged away from my guts and starting to regret my decision. Then when they dressed my skinless body in bandages I was placed in a waiting room before the Big Surgery, and I was trying to find a way to tell my parents that I'd changed my mind. I didn't want to be cut in half and put back together, and I was distraught because my skin had been removed and my skin is quite lovely to touch, being soft n' all, and I thought I'd done something irrevocable.

Then I was confused about why I'd wanted to be shorter, and why I was willing to risk the severance of my spine to achieve that aim. And I felt so guilty for changing my mind because the support of my parents = I'd wasted their time and emotion.

I don't much like having my skin removed. Plus I'm old enough to start shrinking soon anyway. Couldn't I have just waited? And what's wrong with average height? I love average! I wish I was average everything!

Anyway, *The End*. Except for the dark resonance, I think that's gonna keep going.

The Also-Baffling Inner Workings of...
...the real world. This has sort-of happened to me twice now.

I was driving home from the studios yesterday afternoon, down a big hill in the far-right lane in an 80 zone, when I noticed the truck driver in the next [middle] lane waving his hands at me.

A bit dangerous, but I looked over properly and realised he was waving hello, friendly, and a bit weird. So I gave a hesitant wave back and looked away. Because I was driving, duh, and had to watch the road. But he kept waving, and when I looked again he was pointing and motioning for me to pull over. I thought shit, I must have a flat tyre or something and he's trying to help me out. So he let me move in front of him, I pulled over and sure enough, he pulled in behind me.

He got out of his truck and came to my window, where I sat waiting because I wasn't gonna get out of the car. And he said: *'I just wanted to say hello... you look nice...'*, and that was it. First of all I sighed with relief because I can't afford another car expense (just got new battery), and then I was kinda amused and surprised. I talked to him for a minute and then he said *'Have you got time to spend five minutes?'*. I said no, *'I have to get a few things for my son'*. Which was the right thing to say because it made me sound very married.

So he left, veered onto the tollway while I drove ahead. Now I wonder if there's some kind of movement going on with trucky/tradies on the internet, where they've discovered they can pick up by getting women's attention on the road, and report back to an audience each time they score? Because the first time it happened it was a guy in a van, who also had that really attractive kind of happy manner about him, only I was confused and trying to work out if I knew him and didn't pull over.

After the confusion comes anger, because it's *dangerous* distracting drivers on a busy road just because your dick wants something from them.

And yet, as I was driving I'd been thinking very specifically about sex. There being this other man, who I've only slightly met, who has me intrigued enough to borrow him for sexual fantasies. Plus it was sunny and hot and I was wearing a skirt and my body was thrumming with an innocent kind of lust. So I wonder what I would have done if I'd had more time to think, and if there'd been somewhere discreet to go nearby.

I don't sleep with strangers, and I didn't really want to cheat on my fantasy, but ya know? What if I could be that kind of woman? If I'd had the book-ishly packaged condom that I'd gotten for free from the counter at a Readings store over a year ago still in my bag – from whence it was only recently removed – would that have changed things?

I'd quite like to have sex with a real penis for a change. What a pity I need it to be attached to somebody I can actually talk to.

Thursday, 15th March, 2012.

!!!!

Ohmigawd – it's already 1 pm and I haven't written a novel OR created a masterpiece. Where does the time go???

Wednesday, 20th March, 2012.

I Dazzled a Someone!

Still in the spirit of small thoughts, because I don't have time for the big ones, I've dragged myself away from the mirror, where I've been trying to see the back of my head, because a woman at the supermarket approached me while I was standing over the bananas, tapping me on the arm to say *'I just have to tell you you have the most beautiful hair – absolutely beautiful...'*, and then walked away.

I used to be told that all the time, even though I'm a ranga, so to hear it now when I'm doubting my possession of redeeming features is kinda nice. Because of course by having beautiful hair I could easily be mistaken for a beautiful person, so there's hope for me yet.

Now back to the drawing table, where it's the insides that matter. Being so deep is a pain in the arse.

Thursday, 22nd March, 2012.

I Waited, I Saw, I Pleased

I waited n' waited and today I couldn't wait anymore so instead of going to the 2 pm session I did what I've done for the past two days, giving in to a very serious case of art-angst by not doing what I'm supposed to be doing, and going to the 11 am session of *The Hunger Games*. And *whoa*. I'm ready to see it again already.

I have no idea if I love the movie or not. I just know I love the story, and was happy to re-live it as live action.

There were moments I thought were rushed, like the reaping scene where the hand gesture was made = one of the most profound moments, give it a second more to linger and have an impact, would you? And the cameras did that woozy thing where they rush you through movement without letting you focus, or zoom in too close, I presume to disorient us in order to make the scene unsettling but really, to me it just looked like bad cinematography.

And so many of the nuances of the story that could have been accommodated weren't accommodated. If you've read the book that doesn't matter because it influences your understanding, so that you cry [I cried!] when Rue's stuck with a pin even though there wasn't much time spent on building their relationship. Those nuances are glaringly absent in places, but I guess she [Suzanne Collins, author] was trying to keep it simple when she converted it to film.

Doesn't matter. I feel replete, and yet hungry for more. No pun intended (seriously, I hate it when that happens and if I wasn't rushing I'd re-think and re-write that sentence). Goodnight.

Tuesday, 27th March, 2012.

Missing the Boat
The one that's sailed without me. To miss the boat of your own life is a tragic thing. But I can't for the life of me think of how to get onto it.

What am I even supposed to be doing? The most angsty week of art making I've ever, ever experienced. Neurons in my brain firing when I look at the things that excite me. But I can't make myself do what I need to do. So I work sluggishly.

It's occurred to me that maybe I'm not even an artist. Maybe I'm just a looker at-er-er of art. The most useless kind of looker-at-er-er in the world, because it doesn't transmute. Because what's the point. At the end of each day life's still the same as it was that morning. I can't make anything happen. Some kind of will missing. Or maybe just misplaced.

Where did I put the damn thing?

———

April 2012

Sunday, 1st April, 2012.

Hot n' Steamy

Small bits of belonging happening all over the place. For example, the sauna. I intended to try this particular pool out as a one-off because it's not exactly close to home, but I keep going back. Partly for the bliss of the swim – I know its quiet times and love its soft water. And its dim lighting. But also because of the sauna, the only sauna I've ever been to where the conversation is so interesting I'd keep going back for more.

Don't take this the wrong way, but I really wish we were allowed to be naked in the sauna.

There are a few men in particular I love talking to. They're so friendly it's easy to join in and get other people joining in, and actually no matter who's there the atmosphere's amazing.

Last Sunday night one of my favourite sauna men came in for the last five minutes of opening time and we launched straight into social politics without any conversational foreplay, and it was one of the most satisfying conversations I've had with strangers for a long time.

The most interesting thing about this is the access it gives me to the way people from different walks of life think. That's invaluable; without interaction across the divide [so to speak], ideas can't be applied. They become exclusive, which is depressing.

I'm trying to say that it was real world stuff, and I was able to share in it without feeling like a tosser. We don't always speak highfalutin' like that; sometimes it's relationships, children, movies, local politics and so on. So it doesn't matter how often we talk about serious things, it just matters that we talk. And that acquaintances can sometimes be as important as friends.

How can I take out a membership at the city pool as planned, when I love going to this one so much? What if the city people aren't friendly? I suppose I can make them friendly, seeing as I talk to anybody within a five-metre radius. But still. I won't necessarily get that feeling of belonging. Ironic, considering I'm not a local.

I'm still lonely, is the problem. I have so many friends, but no intimacy. No companionship. These tiny, condensed moments where there's concentrated talking add something beautiful to my day.

The End of The Loneliness Era, Please?
Loneliness be damned. The more I'm in the [Art Skool] world the more welcome I feel. The friendships are concrete, and people seek me out. People whose names I can't remember approach me and tell me they were talking about me with other, newer friends of mine, so that I know my presence is sinking into the social landscape. A veritable ink spillage. So even though I've wasted a lot of energy worrying about how I'm tripping over my words because I'm juggling so many concepts at once, I know that in some way I'm making sense.

I have to force myself out of the habit of assuming that everything I do is stupid, exacerbated over the past few horrible years, as a by-product of being unloved. I remind myself that misery is selfish, because it makes you so scared of being in the way that you forget how to relax with people. When you exercise your fears you're concentrating on how awful *you* are, instead of enjoying people fully for who *they* are.

So now I officially don't give a rats; am just going to go about my business and enjoy everything n' everyone around me. Because I can.

Or Not
The Biological came to visit his offspring last week. This was a significant event because it hasn't happened for a while. He called a few days earlier and we had a long catch up, which was really nice. He had that love in his voice, which was also nice. Said he wanted to drop in and see me, which is not so nice, because I know that means sex for him where it means something entirely different for me, and because he never calls first and I'm way too busy to give him as much time as he takes up.

But still, nice. When he came to pick First-Born up for a driving lesson – in a vintage American convertible with left-hand steering and no seatbelts [!!!] – I was really happy to see him. He found me downstairs, bent over a board covered in drawing panels, with inky paint brushes in my hand. I stood up and he hugged me tightly, with gropey affection, so that I felt his hands moving around my body in a loving act of remembering. I nearly cried, because I haven't been touched by a human being for a very, very long time.

First-Born clearly didn't want him hanging around with the likes of me so off they went, to do their dangerous driving. And I was left with that reminder. I have to remedy this emptiness. Not with him, but with somebody. I hug a lot of people, but not like that. You can't go for this long without love in your life, it's just not healthy. I miss it bad.

On that subject, I found this in my March notebook:

> *The secret to being happy is to not sit around thinking about how unhappy you are;*
>
> *Even though I'm a happy person, I've failed to make a happy life;*
>
> *Is being out in the world constantly really happiness, or is it just a distraction from the empty life you have to return to every night?;*
>
> *To be happy I need to be writing that story. Then I can worry about filling life up again. As long as I have the story everything else will be okay.*

Friday, 6th April, 2012.

Another Ketchup in Small Parts

Oh Lawdy. *Teenagers.* This time it's Grandkitten, who for the past three nights has insisted on going outside at night and then hasn't come back in.

Out all night! Like a common cat! I hope she doesn't keep doing this. And if I smell booze and cigarettes on her fur there'll be trouble.

I miss the little creature. She belongs at my feet. Where I don't have to worry about her.

Have Locomotive, Will Travel

I've finally done it; I've conquered a fear and [re-]started catching the train in to the city. I am, naturally, triumphant. Because I had to change the way I think; stop being Little Black Rain Cloud who focuses on the negative (motor tic = physical discomfort, crowds, sore neck), and start being Little Ray of Sunshine who focuses on the positive.

There are a million kinds of freedom to be enjoyed when you catch the train. First of all there's the wind up your skirt; all of that city air circulating around your thighs as you walk from one destination to another is a very pleasant thing.

One thing you don't do when you drive is walk between destinations. I like it. I love it. You feel part of the city, then. And not tied to your vehicle. I'm also free because my time isn't limited to parking restrictions. I don't have to keep returning to my car. If I want to stay longer I can, and I do.

The best studio conversations happen at both the beginning and the end of the day. I forgot about this. Now I'm there for them, and I feel more at home. And the direct sunlight, at this time of year, is hidden by large buildings when I leave in the evening. Shade! This makes for ranga-friendly habitat. Shade + wind up my skirt = a good day. (Motor tic = sore neck, though. Maybe I'll acclimatise?)

Thursday, 12th April, 2012.

Fuck. Fuck *fuck fuck fuck fuck*.

I've been wide awake since 5:30 am, which is normally okay because I'm out walking the hills by then. My body knows this. I tried to sleep in today because I can't stand my life and First-Born keeps me awake 'til all hours and when I finally sleep I inevitably get woken and so on and so on. So, a sleep-in, only my body decides it wishes it were walking the hills and my skin wants to feel the bite of cold air and then First-Born gets up again and it's all noise and I'm so fucking wide awake I could cry.

The angst is back. Obviously. My mind's racing so I'm forcing myself to sit here and dump every stinking thought I can squeeze out. It's no good lying awake at night torturing yourself with full-force acknowledgement of your emptiness unless you're going to fix it.

A Little Think

So, this man. It's hard to concentrate on some things when there's a man in your head. Such as when you're walking and you play your writing music on the iPod but then give in and flick it over to a playlist full of love songs. Oh *fuck off*.

What's gotten into me? Do I have a crush on him? It's possible. I do want to be naked with him. Because he said some nice things about nakedness and he said them in a very nice way. Naturally, that's where my mind went. Not his intention, but still, it's nice to be curious even though there's no way in hell that curiosity will go anywhere.

Especially seeing as I hardly know him, and when I get to know him I'll discover that his saying lovely things on the outside does not mean he's beautiful on the inside. Plus he wears black socks with shorts, a sure sign of ugly insides.

For now, though, I like him. I like him *that way*. It's about time I had somebody real to wonder about. Until somebody more accessible comes along. Because seriously, I have shit loads of work to do and I have no time for this.

Thought-Dump #1

Art. Do I even like it anymore? I ask myself this question a lot. I'm addicted to it, I love the studios [do I?], and the research, and it's no secret that I live and breathe the stuff. It's one of my chosen vehicles for thought. But *so what?*

It seems like less of a beautiful world to be part of than it could be, sometimes. An example: Young Studio Friend, who everybody loves.

I can't even tell you why. I'm lucky that we're friends. But for the first time, about a month ago, I was really disappointed in her. I wanted to tell her but never got the chance. And how do you do that anyway?

One of the other studio youngins from our year, who graduated last year (remembering that I'm a doddering old thing one year behind my original peers) was having her first exhibition opening. This is a big deal. Exhibition openings are what we do. We go to them. All of us, if we can. I assumed we'd always do this, take an interest in what each other is doing. And this young woman is particularly present at all of the events. She's supportive, and she's sincere.

So when Young Studio Friend said she couldn't be bothered going, and that she thought it'd be shit anyway because it was a commercial gallery (i.e. how uncool) I was really upset. Because that was irrelevant; what mattered was that we support this friend by being there. And why dismiss her work so harshly? Why be so transparently elitist? Is attending openings about scoring points, or enjoying the shared experience of being artists?

What's troubling me is that when you get to a certain point, there's no joy left in art. It's all about performing the fitting of in. You have to fight to keep your integrity, and you have to fight to keep the cool people's eyes open to the false nature of coolness.

The things that were making me feel joyful have been kicked out of everybody, and we have to get them back.

Thought-Dump #2

I started a group. I didn't mean to. It's just that I get these ideas and I tend to sit on them because I think they should be thunk and acted upon by people stronger than myself. This time I didn't sit on the idea; I said it out loud to some studio friends, on Day One of the studio year.

Within a week the idea became a group of people working together on collaborative projects, and we're up n' running. The shape of the thing changed (it always does within a group) and I adjusted. All good.

So anyway, I think this might be an avenue for restoring the missing joy. If I can learn not to take myself too seriously. Maybe lighten the fuck up.

Thought-Dump #3
Seriously? Is this my idea of a pep talk? Because it's a bit pitiful. But here goes nothing:

I need to write. This isn't a whim, this is something I have to do. Just quietly, like here, banging away at things without anybody watching.

To do this I need sleep, and sleep is my biggest problem, because of First-Born's nocturnalness. MUST FIND A WAY AROUND IT.

In the meantime, I have to be monastic. I have to function. Because if I can't force out what's inside then I'm nothing. I feel like nothing. Hence the emptiness.

And I have to make sure that, when in the studio, I'm doing what matters to me, and doing it in a way that matters. Must bleed the poison out. And start again. Because for all of this serious stuff I'm working on, I'm not getting very much done.

Thought-Dump #4
Maybe I'm not getting as much done as I need to because I'm working without a defined goal. Everything's part of something but there's no overall shape.

This is an Einstein moment. Defined goal! Of course!

Note to self: *define your goals*.

Thought-Dump #5
Bullshit. There's no shape because I'm doing too many things. Doing too many things is the same as doing nothing. I am, how you say, overwhelmed.

Still, define goals. Jettison what's too hard. Roger that.

Thought-Dump #6
In my notebook: Germaine. Whatever I mean by that.

Friday, 13th April, 2012.

Thought-Dumping, Continued in Miserable Fashion

Something to look forward to. When I get like this it's because there isn't anything. I can't see a future and therefore can't aim for it. Because today is yesterday's future, and it's no different from today's yesterday, which creates a pattern that tells me that today's future could be just as empty, and is actually likely to be because the things I'm doing now aren't promoting change.

And because I'm not writing. The future I want involves story. Art's there, too, but it can't exist for me without story. So I know I need to write, but can't foresee the quiet needed for writing. I have to find a way to be a mushroom and still be a functioning, social, artist-y being.

The only thing I enjoy is swimming. I wish I could do it every day.

It's so hard to live without love. Love and a good night's sleep. Nothing makes life better. Everything I do just keeps me busy. The end of every day is still the same.

―――

A Letter from First-Born

They left it for me on top of the clunky old typewriter I bought the other day. It's a beautiful old machine. And I drove not far from here to get it. Isn't it amazing that you can look something up on-line, ring somebody, and within five minutes be on their doorstep to buy it. Well, maybe ten minutes. But within five minutes I was driving the back roads, and discovered that the pretend country is so close to me I could sneeze on it. If I wanted to. Unmade roads where you pass teenagers riding horses. Surrounded by farms. All quiet-like.

Anyways, the letter. It's a nice letter. I read it after a night of tossing and turning, during which they'd woken me six times. I hate being in my bed, and my bedroom, and this house. When I got up, late, before I found the letter, I opened the curtains and all of that lovely sun came pouring in from the north, and the memory of happiness here just hit me. Because this house used to be full of happiness, and life.

The letter. I'll think on it later. It hasn't made me feel any happier, but it really is nice. Monumentally. First-Born signed off with *'So cheer up n' shit...'* which made me laugh. But still. No sleep. I'm wrecked and can't see a way past the wreckedness.

Wednesday, 18th April, 2012.

It Got Better

Just saying. Happy again. Yay. Weird, but yay. It's always about the possibility of the emptiness being filled, isn't it. As long as the possibilities are kept open.

And I'm out in the world, doing things that lead Elsewhere every day. If I just had a bit o' patience, yes? And if I get on with the job. There's a good girl.

If you'd told me as recently as half a year ago that I'd happily spend hours kicking back on the couch with a cup of green tea, doing embroidery, I wouldn't have believed you.

Saturday, 21st April, 2012.

The Ghost Chronicles

First-Born said *Good Morning* to me this morning, and now that they're being nice I don't want them to. This because I accidentally eavesdropped on my offspring two nights ago. I don't usually accidentally eavesdrop; I usually do it on purpose. Not usually to them, but sometimes.

That was my first act of ghostness, only I didn't know it then. Like being invisible and walking through walls.

Anyway. I'd gone to bed early. Eight-thirty early. I was run down and exhausted and thought that was my chance to get up early AND have a good night's sleep. I haven't had unbroken sleep for well over a month, and you can see it on my face. Without sleep I'm a true ye olde. So I used earplugs, and I left them to it.

I knew they were in the kitchen, talking, because I couldn't fall asleep. I tried to relax, with the murmur of their voices but no words reaching me down in my room. Then eventually I got up to very innocently and uneavesdroppingly go to the loo, not because I needed to but because I thought maybe if I do something ritualistic, like pee, I'd be able to fall asleep. So I took my earplugs out and tiptoed out of my room, not wanting them to stop talking because them spending time together = a nice thing.

What a nice mother I am. But only a bit nice. I hesitated at the bottom of the stairs when I realised they were talking about me. About how annoying I am [!!]. I was amused at first, because all they could come up with was that my bedroom's in a stupid place, that I should have chosen a different room, and that I'm noisier than I think I am, oh *ha ha ha*. That one got a laugh from them and raised eyebrows from me, on accounta First-Born was complaining that I wake them up at 5 am and then again at 8 am, which disturbs their sleep patterns. I don't think I could find a bigger irony if I tripped over it.

They also both hate it when I knock on their bedroom doors. For your big fat information, I also hate knocking on their doors. I hate it absolutely. But it's the only way I ever get to speak to them, and there are things I have to tell them, like *I'm going to work can you please put cat #3 outside when she wakes up*, or *I'm going for a walk (i.e. you have the house to yourself for an hour, enjoy)*, or *your dinner's ready*, or *can you please put your washing in the machine*, or *I'm going to bed please be quiet goodnight*; all practical things.

I don't knock on First-Born's door often because history has taught me not to. We text each other when something has to be said, which is half sad and half hilarious. But anyway, it works.

Now I want to start texting Son instead of going into his room, seeing as I'm so unwelcome, but how do I tell him to keep his phone nearby without telling him I heard what they were saying and that this is my solution?

Son, who isn't a bad kid, won't come out to the kitchen or lounge room if I'm there. One day recently, when his friends were here, he wouldn't sit down to eat with them because I was talking to them. A tiny example to illustrate how unwelcome I am. But you'll notice that I'll be driving his girlfriend home again [as usual] late on Sunday night – he doesn't mind me being around for that.

So bugger them both. I don't like being at home with them, and I don't want to talk to them anymore. I know it's normal to want distance from your parents, but I'm sensitive about it because I do so much invisible work to keep their lives running smoothly and to make sure that our relationships don't crumble under the strain of the evil past. It's not fair that I should be the unwelcome one.

And, to put it bluntly, apart from a token gesture here and there from either of them, I do all of the housework. *All of it.* Seeing as they think the machine that keeps the world running is so annoying to have around, I don't want them to say good morning or goodnight or to talk to me at all. Until they grow the fuck up.

Sunday, 22nd April, 2012.

Half Off the Hook, Sort Of Maybe

When he was young I used to love that the first thing Son did when he got up in the morning was come to see me. He'd find me, and then he'd go about his business. I was the thing to orbit around.

Now I don't know whether to think of him as Good Son or Bad Son.

Yesterday he got up and got his breakfast and then disappeared into his room. I didn't speak to him until I had to knock on his door in the evening to tell him that I was going for a swim. Yes! I had to knock on his door! Fucken fuck. The first thing I said was *'Good morning Mother, lovely day, isn't it?'*, at which he cringed.

By the time I was going to bed I'd had to knock on his door about five times, and now that I'm even more self-conscious about being unwelcome I made it sound like my idea when I told him I hate knocking on his door and I'm going to send him texts from now on. He told me *No, that's silly,* said he was talking to First-Born about it a couple of days ago and it's only annoying at certain times. I thought *Oh, that's a bit nice,* and removed him from my bad books. [Good Son.]

But then he went straight back into my bad books again, because he's going to see *The Hunger Games* with his girlfriend today, and I asked him if he's read the book, which I bought for him and have been asking him to read for over a year, and he said *Yes.* He had in fact read it within a day of my ramming it at him at the beginning of the holidays, weeks ago, when I told him the cinema experience has to include the book experience so you *have to* read it, and then give it to your girlfriend to read, too.

So, he lives with his lovely mother, who happens to be *excited about it*, and yet Son didn't think it was worth a conversation when he'd read the book I cared so much about him enjoying. It mattered to me that he read it, and he knew that it mattered.

I told him he sucks. And now, twelve hours later, I still think he sucks. [Bad, *Bad Son*.]

Sunday, 22nd April, 2012.

Drawn and Quartered

Maybe I'm a hundred years behind the eight ball, and I did know that art has its own mind-frame in the same way that writing has its mind-frame, and that it's not the least bit easy to switch between one and the other. I even compare the process of making art to the process of writing ALL THE TIME. As in, *this piece of work's like a short story*, and *this one's like writing a novel*. I think I measure them by intensity of experience. But – it wasn't until a couple of days ago that I realised the thought processes are also exactly the same. And that's because I'm trying to re-enter the novel.

I *have* re-entered the novel, but the art thoughts are competing and kind of winning. I haven't managed the divide I wanted. I don't know if it's because I've introduced a narrative quality to my art, which excites me no end, that the story of the pieces I'm working on plays over and over inside my mind the way a novel will play over and over. Usually it's the chapter-in-progress at the time, over and over until the way forward is presented and you have to find your way to a computer with some urgency.

The long think is the same. I'm baffled by this. It means that I'm writing two novels at once, albeit one with a combination of words and images. Art cheats to win my affection because I get to use colour. So writing's hard work plus playful imagination plus more hard work, but this art I'm doing is like writing with hard work plus playful imagination plus more hard work AND chocolate.

This is a problem. Because I need them both, and I can try to be two people, but I only have one brain. (Fuck.)

Today I'll write. I'll write I'll write I'll write. And then art. The divide has to be found, and I *will* find it.

Monday, 23rd April, 2012.

Twenty-Four Minus...

I love this. This is the world I want to be in, the one where I can buy a book and be lost in it for hours without feeling guilty about the time, and then wander off and be lost in one of my own making, also not feeling guilty about that time. There's a rightness to it.

So I was thinking, there are twenty-four hours in a day. Even if I sleep for eight of them (if I could actually sleep), there'll still be sixteen hours left. Minus two or three for getting in and out of the city and a couple for potting around, feeding children and cats, there are still twelve hours left. Minus one for walking. That's five hours for writing, and six for art. If I catch the train instead of driving – motor tic be damned – I can spend the two travelling hours reading.

Vary the schedule for when I want to swim, and for gardening, and going to work... fuck. Maybe if I make four different schedules, keep the above reckoning as my primary and the others for days with extra in them. I'll work this out. My inner mathematician will get it right and life will be peachy.

Wednesday, 25th April, 2012.

A Happy Accident

Son asked me to buy a copy of *The White Tiger* for his ex-girlfriend, for her birthday, which is really funny when you think about how he doesn't remember to buy his lovely mother a birthday present BUT ANYWAY. I did buy it, but because I'm an adult who loves a good story and not a teenage girl who loves fantasy, I assumed he meant Aravind

Adiga, because what other *White Tiger* could there possibly be in the literary world? And then because I hadn't read it before I thought I should open it to see if it's okay, because I didn't want him giving her a broken book or anything.

That was it, love at first sight. I had to buy another copy for her, and keep this one, seeing as I'd made love to it already. Only, when I searched the bookshops to find it I noticed the other *White Tiger*, the Kylie Chan one, and realised what an enormous divide there is between my world and the younginses.

I'm going to talk Son into reading it, to see what he thinks. It's not enough that he loves *those* books, I want him to love *these*. Because if I were to write a one-word review of the thing it would simply say '*Perfect*'.

———

Monday, 30th April, 2012.

Oh Grow Up

I know the example I'm about to give makes me the fusty old grown up in a world full of hip young people, but I have to say that people who don't think past the surface make the world so ugly sometimes.

I was listening to the radio after dropping Son off at school, and Lehmo was telling Brig about the discovery that he-who-shall-not-be-named (Os Bin L) used Viagra and Just for Men hair dye. He thought it was hilarious and was cracking puerile jokes about multiple and young wives in classic I-didn't-mature-past-adolescence style, and it just plain old wasn't funny. It made me think of the corpses of slain enemies left hanging on Medieval city gates to decompose in public.

I read a book last year that included an essay-ish thing written by OBL, and of course I don't believe in his methods, but he was very articulate re his ideological stance. His viewpoint was one that could be considered both seriously and respectfully. He was a human being who cared about something sincerely. It would've been nice if he hadn't blown people up to make his point, but still.

I don't know. It just seemed wrong to try to ridicule somebody who's part of something so big and serious. It wasn't satire; satire would have been okay. It was just stupid and ignorant.

Why was that kind of information released anyway? I already know the answer; for people like Lehmo to get a kick out of. The Mighty West doing its victory lap.

World. Ugly. Told you so.

May 2012

Tuesday, 8th of May, 2012.

Unwanted Cause to Debrief

An exasperated sigh. Churchy Friend often does this. Something festive is coming up, and she'll say something negative about me or to me that throws a wet blanket over the whole thing, so that I can't quite enjoy it fully.

Just over two Xmases ago, when we'd invited her to join our family on a trip to the High Plains for My Lovely Mother, Churchy Friend made some disparaging remarks about how inadequate I was as a human being, for arriving late. I already felt bad, like I was letting people down, as I constantly did, but I texted her the following week to explain. My explanation included an incident I'd had to handle at home, which was incredibly dramatic and traumatic, not to be taken lightly. At that time I had nobody to consult or reassure or advise me. I was broken, is the point, and profoundly, debilitatingly sad.

That sparked off a string of e-mails with Churchy Friend telling me how she (a youth worker) couldn't handle hearing about that kind of thing and aren't I a horrible person for burdening her with such trifles and so on. The friendship ended there. Long e-mails where she said horrible things and I suggested she just accept that she doesn't like me and let's leave it at that.

And then I went about the miserable business of this painful parenting experience, even more alone than ever. Because even though I hardly told her any of the details, she was the only person I spoke to about it.

Today, with Son's eighteenth birthday approaching, she sends me texts telling me frankly that I'm awful for not rushing home to be with him on the day, as though I'm being selfish, because she wanted to come to dinner earlier than I intend to be there.

Actually, First-Born and I have tried to talk Son into celebrating and he refuses. We've put a lot of thought into how we'll handle the event. I explained this to Churchy, via text. She said *'Cool'*. Then she messaged First-Born and tried to organise something behind my back, telling First-Born that it's because I'm *not a very good mother* (not in those words). i.e. She tried to HIJACK my kids.

First-Born, in a moving display of loyalty to me and quite frankly insulted by Churchy Friend's misunderstanding of Son's ways and the way we handle our domestic situation, showed me what Churchy had written and then messaged Churchy back, telling her she was offending both of us.

Anyhoo, First-Born said it so affectionately and tactfully that I was really proud of them. Then I emailed a letter to Churchy, explaining, and have been given the royal *Fuck You*.

I made the mistake of asserting my right to respond. Because we've been to hell and back in this household, and I've held us together, at great emotional cost. And I know Son better than she does; what he wants, and what he can handle. Things she'd have no idea about because she consciously opted out.

Anyway, I tried to communicate with her sincerely and kindly, but so far the *Fuck You* stands. So is this another end I wonder, of our friendship? Alone again. Naturally.

Monday, 14th May, 2012.

Hip Hip... Hooray?

Well, Son has turned eighteen, and I made it all the way through a walk and into the shower that morning before crying. Yey me. Yey me also for raising my children safely into adulthood.

[*I have adult children !!!!!*]. It was meant to be a happy occasion but he refuses to celebrate. *Too much school work*, he said, but it's my job to worry so wot they hey.

When I was in the kitchen at breakfast-time, having just made the fudge-which-is-really-ganache I always make for them for special occasions, and wrapping the roll of money I was about to give him in happy red ribbon, he did something that made me cry again, even though I shouldn't take it personally. He got his sandwich things out of the fridge and the cupboard, he got a plate and knife, and he left the room with them. He took them into his bedroom to make his lunch, because he doesn't like me being around when he's getting ready for school. He also can't stand me being around when he gets home from school. If I'm in the kitchen he'll wait until I'm gone before he comes out to get food.

Well *of course* I had to cry again. Motherhood is devastating. But I'm training myself to not let the sad things dominate my thoughts, because it's counterproductive. My job is to make happy things happen, that being the only way to push the sad things out.

I failed at this recently because I went on strike again. When I go on strike you know about it instantly in this house; I'm like the council garbage collection and if I don't turn up the streets are strewn with litter. I forgot that the one thing I need to keep doing is make our home life run as smoothly as possible against the odds, so that we have an illusion of normality to delude ourselves with. Son relies upon this, even though what I do to maintain this illusion is largely invisible to him. I absorb the shock before it hits him. Inasmuch as I can.

So when I went on strike he got stressed. I was so busy feeling my own stress, I didn't anticipate his. Son's rationale for his refusal to help is that First-Born doesn't help, therefore it's not fair for him to help. When I counter this with *'But by not helping you're leaving it all for me'* he shrugs his shoulders because compassion for your mother doesn't override issues of sibling fairness. There's no such thing as parental fairness, due to the pervasive concept of parental sacrifice.

When I realised how stressed he was by the mess, I had to become self-sacrificial all over again. It's just another reminder that we have no control over how we live, and I don't want him to be reminded of this. I felt so guilty, seeing the sense of hopelessness I let fill the house and his head by leaving the mess where it was.

He's eighteen, but he's at school until the end of the year. This means I still have time to salvage the last part of his childhood. Make the last months good. Or at least smooth. I have to be the invisible force that holds the walls up.

I mourn the loss of the second part of his childhood. I mourn for it all the time. So to hold the walls up I have to hide my emotions, even when he leaves the room because I've walked into it. We get along well generally, this is just a quirk of his. Don't take it personally, Mother. Make happy things happen. Then sit back and wait for them [see above] to push the sad things out.

———

June 2012

―――

Wednesday, 20ᵗʰ June, 2012.

Kickin' Back
It's tragic that the thing I most look forward to when it comes to the holidays between semesters is being able to do a lot more work. Elbow deep in the stuff, and lovin' it.

―――

Friday, 22ⁿᵈ June, 2012.

Gotcha!
I did what must count among the most stupid things I've ever done in my life. I fell into the local career criminal's conversation trap and I fell bad. He now knows where I live.

I've met him before, a few times. I hate being a blip on his radar, but because I walk all the time he knows me and my movements. So he caught me for our first proper conversation a long time ago, told me roughly where I lived (no idea how he would know that), and asked me for my house number. He's so friendly, which binds you into a social contract that you feel impolite breaking. He asks a lot of questions, and throws that one in. The first time I didn't tell him, I out-clevered him by deflecting it. But last night he caught me off-guard, and I said my house number.

What was going through my head: *Maybe he already knows, and if I lie he'll think I'm scared; If I don't answer this question, he'll think I'm scared of him; I might offend him if he really is just being friendly; If I could just remember what I told him last time...* etc. A complex but split-second line of thought that led me to answer because of that damn social contract. I was, in effect, demonstrating a weakness (social kindness), and have labelled myself as somebody to manipulate. I should at the very least have told him *'That's an inappropriate question'*. At the very most, to just fuck off. Two statements that all people should be taught to practise, so that we have it in our conversational arsenal.

He also made comment about me being comfortable walking at night, and asked me where I walked. I could see the mechanism of his mind during that conversation. Offering me his details so that I'd offer mine to him. And he ended the conversation with *'Sleep well'*, which is downright creepy once you've given him your house number.

Fuck. Now, instead of loving my hillside, I have to be vigilant. I can no longer walk at night, or alone. This is no small deal; walking's an enormous element of my life, every single day, rain or shine. The only thing that stops me is high wind (falling trees). And local career criminals, apparently.

I'm angry, but that just reveals to me what a golden age of walking in the dark I've had. I'm a female animal, so technically I shouldn't feel safe anywhere. Society gives an illusion of safety, and improves the level of safety, but it doesn't eliminate danger and I'm always telling people not to forget that.

Fucken fucken *fuck*. One of the best things in my life has been ruined. Living here has been ruined. All because I felt I had to be polite. Motherfucking prick. I'm a blip on his radar AND a sitting duck. Not fucking likely. The first thing I have to do is confront him. Tell the police, and my VIP executive policeman brother. And then what. Something. I'll think of something good.

July 2012

Sunday, 1st July, 2012.

Wow.
I've been reading through my blog entry files, trying to see if I can find reference to the first time I was approached by the local career criminal, because I need to go to the police again to tell them something that might relate to a local investigation but that's so vague it probably doesn't, and it'd be good if I could give solid facts as opposed to speculative observations, just in case.

I couldn't find that information, and I know that's because instead of writing it into a blog entry I saved it up for a literary piece I ended up writing late last year.

Anyhow, whenever I start reading these files I keep reading, it being the book-of-my-life so to speak and therefore interesting to me if to nobody else. I didn't realise, until now, how much I write about writing and art. [So much!] For the moment I won't let it bother me how indicative this is of how little other life I have; instead I'm wow-ing because it turns out the things I've written about writing and art are actually very useful to me. Even when I forget them.

Which just goes to show how effective the brain-dumping process is; you write, you forget, you move on without mental burden. It pays to be simple minded.

Monday, 2nd July, 2012.

Game of Boring-Old-Betrayal n' Such
Because my reward for a hard semester's work was to watch *Game of Thrones I* [again] and *II* [for the first time] for two days running a couple of weeks ago, I was hunkered down with my arty handcrafts

[needle n' thread] in front of the tv. That's why I thought of my thimble as Finger Armour. Why I still think of my thimble as Finger Armour.

I don't know what to think of the second series. Seemed a bit too much of the same thing over n' over, with repetitive betrayal and intrigue n' wot not. When I expressed this to Dad he said *'Yes, it was a bit like a soapie'*. Which is funny, because in my notebook I'd described it as *Bold and the Beautiful* with helmets.

I put up with that for the most part, but it lost me with the birth of that shadow creature from the red woman's bits. I remember saying out loud *'Oh that's just stupid'*. Yes, yes it is. You can take fantasy too far, and if it's too high-fantasy I don't like it. Dragons are good because they have a lore built up to support their imaginary existence; start introducing weak magic and it's just a plot cop-out, a too-easy way out of a situation.

So I was planning not to watch the next series, but that final scene with the white walkers has me hooked. NOW I HAVE TO WAIT A WHOLE NOTHER YEAR!

I wonder if I can wear my thimble as jewellery. I'm not much of a jewellery person, beyond plain earrings and leather straps of sorts, but finger armour I could maybe do. Once it's on I really hate taking it off.

Wednesday, 25th July, 2012.

Things That Save Me: Part One

With the shortage of knights in shining armour riding in on their trusty steeds, I'm more than happy to be saved again by stories. Specifically this time, *The Ship Kings* series. Thank the universe for producing Andrew McGahan.

I predicted that the emptiness would hit me again before the holidays had finished, because I'd be spending crazy amounts of time alone. I used to love time alone, but it's only good to be alone if the aloneness is proportionally balanced with time spent with people. And if you're not so distracted by the lack of people that you can't concentrate on the hard work you want to be doing. No need to explain that here. Point is, I'm happy but I fall easily.

I need to hurry up n' fall in love, if I even can. In the meantime, I find these things that fulfill me completely. This book. I picked it up because I'm writing about the ocean. Theoretically writing. Any actual writing happening? Trying to stay motivated, or hopeful, or whatever it is that's died and needs reviving.

The ocean scares me because it's foreign. I need an entry point to really bring it to life. Andrew McGahan's story is quite generic in some ways, the typical Fantasy-genre ways, and at first I found the ye olde language disappointing because it's a characteristic of the Fantasy genre that not enough authors seem to question. And the character relationships are so simplistic it's baffling. But those things hardly mattered. Because the story – well. It's the kind that absorbs you so completely you're transported. I needed that and I needed it bad. It made me the kind of happy I used to always be and will one day soon be again. (WHEN I'M WRITING.)

Most importantly, he made me feel the ocean the way I needed to feel it. He's amazing. I feel like I've discovered a new god. One that's made the world I need to create more possible than it was before. How do you thank somebody for something so profound. How do you even.

Thursday, 26th July, 2012.

Things That Save Me: Part Two

Simple rapture. Climbing the hill up toward the reservoir wall and finding an extraordinarily beautiful sky at the top of it. The whole park to myself because of the strike. (The strike! Somebody has to help our parks!)

I rode high on Andrew McGahan's novel for quite a few days. I saw people and the seeing of people made me happy. I swam many laps. I walked my compromised hillside. But at home, alone, emptiness crept back in. I waited the holidays out, but by the end of them couldn't imagine the world I was going to return to could re-fill the emptiness after all. It was this gaping maw and it had me.

Until that long, rigorous walk, most of it spent crying because I've gone back to that old trick, crying without reason and without much prompting. Then the sky; I laid eyes on it and the peace just fell into me. I felt my face smile. I walked the wall and my phone rang. It was Breeding Studio Friend (can't remember what I usually call her), who I'd visited during the week, who could see through my pretend-happiness (cracking-on-the-verge-of-inexplicable-tears voice being a dead give away, despite my otherwise perfect performance) and was ringing to see if I was okay. She'll never know what it meant to me for her to call me at that moment, up there on the wall, in the middle of my empty sea. Two pure happinesses at once – her, and the water.

That's how life turns around. Not being alone, and the world so pretty. And my body thriving in it. Everything on the verge of good. Any minute now. And counting.

Friday, 27th July, 2012.

Scrub Like Yer Life Depends On It

It turns out I do belong in the bigger world. Entering it again will do that to you. I went into the studios for an exhibition opening and saw some beautiful art. I spoke to beautiful people. My people!

Taking advantage of this return to the world, I thought I'd attempt to return home to the way it was. I've been avoiding this because I knew it'd mean destroying fortified spider habitat in the downstairs bathroom. The most beautiful webbery. I leave the light on down there until bedtime, so that I don't have to use other lights, because I like the house dim at night. I navigate by that light, just like the bugs do when it's warm, such tiny bugs, gazillions of them.

Those big fat black spiders living on the other side of the flyscreen are among the happiest you'll find on the planet. I'm really glad I didn't have to kill them; they tucked themselves in when I removed the screen and scraped away years' worth of spider house-building. The webs were tough and so clumped-together they were sticky and thick like grey fairy floss.

Anyhow, all gone. I cleaned the dust from the shower fan (above), even though I loved its texture. I scrubbed the walls. I scrubbed everything. My bathroom's always clean where it needs to be clean, but now it's also normal. I can see through the window. Beautiful view. Everything's now a bit sterile but I'll get used to it.

I also scrubbed pots and cleaned out the oven. Who cleans out their oven? Seriously? Do people do this all the time? Well. I'm not sure I'm fond of shiny pots, but I'll get used to them, too. Bit by bit, I'll do this house over.

Tonight, my writing students here for dinner. Such a normal thing to do, having people over. It's been a long time since I've done normal things like this. Home matters.

And one more thought. I took one of my students down to the studio with me to find my cutlery box, and she pointed to some paintings and asked *'Is that your work?'* with pleased inflections, and I answered with a simple *yes* and changed the subject. Why do I do that? All of this work and I don't show it to people. As though it's all nothing. That's another step I have to take, bringing it to life and sharing it with people. Because it does matter. And it should matter.

Right then. I need to pull my finger out and get to it. The rest of the scrubbing can wait.

Saturday, 28th July, 2012.

A Conversation

Between First-Born and I, via text massage last night:

>Me: *Are you coming home tonite?*

>First-Born: *Ja, art fags gone?*

>Me: *They were my writing students, and yes they're gone.*

>First-Born: *Same shit, different fag league.*

>Me, for hours afterwards: *laughing!*

Somebody Else's Rapture

Late last year Mum n' I started finding knickers hung up around the reservoir park whenever we went walking. Somebody's trophies. I'd forgotten about them, but have found some more. Kinda funny. Kinda pathetic, yes, but still funny. Although I do worry about the woman, because the knickers are really ugly. Maybe I should leave a note up on the fence telling her that plain black cotton is really sleek, so that she can get over her lace phase. I can't stand the idea of somebody wearing these. Ewww.

August 2012

Saturday, 4th August, 2012.

I love today!
I love every day! My house smells like birthday, because I just blew out candles. We had candles on the dining table with dinner because First-Born's partner bought Thai food for all of us. They're watching *Fight Club* upstairs. Not going out the way they usually do. And ain't it snug, having my little family home. Like this.

We all spent the day with our bigger family, at a park, having a picnic, my niece and nephew over from Tasmania. Kids I love, Feral Brother's kids. He even smiled. I love feral Brother when he smiles, makes him more human, makes him friendly, so anyway I got to hang with the kids, my other nieces and nephews too, one big happy family. We rode the paddle boats, it kills your legs, all that paddling, but what a day. And Son and First-Born and their partner in the car, stopping for hot donuts on the way home. I really love us. I even love the house again. Being here. Working well, the way I used to. I don't know why suddenly. But peaceful, ya know?

So I went swimming tonight, I always go swimming, and Art School's such a good world. And I wrote a short story, very clunky. I'm out of practise but I don't care, because I gave it empty time, the way I need to, dammit I did it, and it felt so good, all of those euphoric texts I sent to Prodigal Friend, I meant them. Even though it sucks. The story. Might have to re-write it. Because I can. Because I want to. Because even when it gets excruciating it's fun.

Also I talked a friend into entering a competition, actually I talked two friends into it, and they both got accepted for the exhibition, and one of them WON it, ten thousand no less. I helped! I did good! It capped off such a good week, and everything's right where it once was wrong, so yes, I love today.

And now reading in bed, perfect for a Saturday night. This is happiness, I can feel it all through my body. Finally.

Monday, 6th August, 2012.

To Self-Censor or Not to Self-Censor…

What do you do when you have an addiction to a particular author, but you don't like one of his books and you want to write why but you hesitate because it's bad manners to do that because what if he – one day – googles himself and there he is reading what you've written, or what if you – one day – are suddenly an actual writer and that means meeting him somewhere writery [by chance] and you have your big-mouthed opinion sitting here as a dirty big secret that makes you trip on your words?

I've voiced this dilemma before; how honest is a body allowed to be?

"He" is Andrew McGahan, and I'm churning through him. But I'm stopping at *White Earth,* with an awful need to be scathing. Because really. It's beautiful to almost-half way, and then the narrative tools he uses to advance the plot get plain old silly. And so synoptic. His agenda is transparently a forging and revisioning of the relationship between human and land, based on an indigenous model. The beautiful thing about that is the relationship's established through story and history. He extends the story to enlighten us about ecology. All noble stuff. But the fiction he's couched it within is a tawdry romance. He relies on mysticism to reinforce the relationship, which also romanticises history. The story becomes a slave to the writer's opinion on important shifts in the world around us. (WHO AM I TO EVEN SAY THIS?)

I'm frustrated. Because as with hippies, this kind of thing defeats the purpose. You can't woo a right-wing thinker with romance. You can't just love a place or an ideology so much that other people will follow you blindly. All of that beautiful insight he has to offer, ruined, because it's not shared in a more honest way. Something less flowery would've been good. Something with more grit. How do you go from *Praise* to this?

Another of his [alleged] crimes (SORRY ANDREW!) is the overdoing of the rich pastoralist angle. The obsession. The crazy unlikelihood of the inheritances – which he acknowledges inside the story itself – lends it all a tasteless air. The giving away of the daughter, something so unrealistic I can't bite at it, let alone chew. And, while I'm at it, he attributes far too much capability to the child. I'm not convinced. His relationship-building is terrible, too. I thought this when reading *Whirlpool* – that he's not very good at making his characters relate to each other. That they move on parallel trajectories instead of crossing paths. But the most fundamental thing, in my big fat opinion, is that aristocracy just isn't interesting when it's so far removed from reality. I can see what he was trying to do, but I wish he'd done it differently.

Anyway. I continued reading because, as stated, I love him. There are wonderful story moments in the thing. They feed my starvation. And I wanted to stay inside his [murky] mind. I skim-read the passages I couldn't stand. Enough to validate my opinions but still continue with the story. And then I read without skimming, through the silly silly ending and on to the epilogue, which is where I wanted him to take me, to the simple romantic conclusion, of human connection between the boy and the cousin.

I want him to write the same book, but to do it with something more real. Because why romanticise our relationship to land when that relationship is already beautiful? Use story, yes. Slow us down. But mysticism? Fuck off. I think he does damage with this story. I think he sends us backwards a million years.

End of opinion. Sorry Andrew McGahan. On a bright note, I'm about to read *Whirlpool* again. Character-relationships be damned, you do good story. Ya big spunk [!!!].

Tuesday, 7th August, 2012.

Speaking of...

...relationship to place, I think I've started moving out of this house mentally. Because I can't walk my hillside with as much freedom now, what with the local career criminal monopolising the landscape. And I can't live in a place where I can't be out in the landscape. Must touch the world I live in. Maybe the answer to where I want to be is halfway between here and the swimming pool. If I live in the area I can walk the hills every day and still swim in my favourite pool, also every day.

It's a bit close to the Bogan Belt, but that's okay. Until I fall in love with somebody elsewhere, it might just have to do. Now I just need about a million dollars to get myself there.

Also Speaking of...

Bogans. Which starts with B, as does Bowling, and Boring, and the word Bigot.

I tried not to swim yesterday, thinking that maybe every day is too much, but in the end I was driven to it. That's my excuse. The thing that drove me there is First-Born's partner. Who I liked a lot the first time they came to visit, but then started to dislike for some inexplicable reason. I think I glimpsed something unpleasant in them and have been trying to overcome the dislike since, because it seems a bit unreasonable on my part.

I'm shocked to realise I'm the evil mother-in-law type. It's just, the thing I think I glimpsed was arrogance. And then I witnessed The Partner bragging (another B) and it made me wince because it made them seem boring. As in, if that's their sum-total then there's not much too 'em. I'm very seriously bored by them.

Then – worse – I found out The Partner bowls. Is even on a Bowling Team. I tried very hard to forgive them for this, but really – *bowling*. No. I can't.

So when they came out with bald bigotry last night, in MY lounge room, it sealed the deal. I really am the evil mother-in-law type. I gave them The Lecture. The bigotry was a single sentence delivered about Muslims and Aborigines. It was a response to my reaction to a news bulletin about the government wanting to introduce full-fee education because subsidies allegedly don't "benefit" general society (short-sighted motherfuckers). First-Born's Partner's government-supporting comment was unforgivable. I should have kicked them out.

Instead I talked about the importance of education on the ground level to eradicate the potential for ignorance, which is the essence of racism. And our country's greed. And the manipulation of the populace. I essentially called them stupid for being so easily manipulated into emotional responses to issues that call for rational understanding.

Twat.

And then I went swimming, in the clean clean water. So that I could talk to my sauna people, one of whom said – when I told him about First-Born's Partner – *'You should bring [them] here, [they] sound like someone who'd use this sauna'*, which is so true.

In the sauna, okay; in my lounge room, not. The sauna represents the common thread of bogan thought, and it must be compartmentalised as such so that it remains manageable. Bigotry MUST NOT LEAK INTO MY LIFE.

What am I going to do about this? Drop notes of disapproval? Remain silent and wait for First-Born to realise their partner's a dick? I know I have to do the latter, but geez, that's a tuff call. Motherhood's difficult even when it's easy.

Saturday, 25th August, 2012.

Like a Duck to Water

Seriously? It's been over two weeks? Well. I'll just add those weeks to the tally of weeks-that-are-fantastic.

I used to be this happy all the time. And it looks like I might be this happy all-the-time again. Maybe forever!

First-Born went for an audition for the leading role in a local theatre company production of that very ace Oscar Wilde play. Not only did they text me to say that they'd nailed it, after being so nervous, but then later when I was at the pool they called to tell me they got the part. And tonight, out for dinner before the younginses left for their night out, I was sitting with the not-so-younginses and First-Born stood beside my seat with their arm over my shoulder. It was such a beautiful and natural gesture. And when I lifted my hand to my shoulder to rest it on theirs, they stayed there.

'Did you see that?' I asked Friend W-L later, and she said *'I did! I didn't want to draw attention to it in case I frightened First-Born away!'*

I love that child. And now I can see them starting to be themself, to really step into the world and be as great as they can be. A very strong personality, an amazing memory for character and voice and dialogue, and a kick-arse sense of humour. First-Born was made for performance. I always thought they'd be a comedian, or an actor of some sort. And now here they are discovering it by accident.

Everyone stops to tell us First-Born's beautiful. When we go out. And now comes the radiance that goes with it, and with fitting into their own skin so comfortably.

My lovely family, all the things I wanted. So happy.

Wednesday, 29th August, 2012.

Fetch Me My Boots

This is going to sound a bit wanky and possibly monotonous, but today I'm willing to declare it out loud. I'm a writer and art's just another vehicle for writing. Yesterday I was such an artist I would have slapped myself for saying so, but really. Lying in the sun by the window today, wishing I was reading a book, but so much art to think about I have no time for reading... it's hard not to resent it. I had to examine that thought and there it was, my singular truth.

Doesn't stop me from reading, I have to say. Last week it was *Foal's Bread*, Gillian Mears, a novel I both loved and didn't like but then loved again once I got to the end. Because it's a really strange and beautiful thing. Poetic, rich, unique, beautifully written. But sometimes put-downable. I know, it doesn't make sense, but that's how it is.

And horses are such beautiful people.

So, writing. I'm so happy generally, but I still miss it. The immersion. I want it back. I can trace all of the things that confuse me about my art practice to that need for story. Repelled by the lack of it. Reluctant to shape myself into something that thinks without it. I'm just not an artist, and I don't want to be one. Those things I'm making are not art. If that's how I define things from now on, I think it'll work. And it gives me permission, which I still seem to need.

The happiness is so *big*. So fuck art. [For now.]

———

September 2012

Saturday, 15th September, 2012.

Oh Dear

I have this new-ish friend, who I met early this year and who I like a lot, as ya do. And I realised after meeting up with her a couple of times that I'd met her before, that she was a friend of Ex-Girlfriend-Not-Girlfriend's. I'd been to her house. About a hundred years ago we applied for the same diploma course and I got in but she went elsewhere. When we'd both applied I really wanted us both to get in, because I liked her so much. She was the only friend of Ex-Girlfriend-Not-Girlfriend's that I thought I could get along with naturally. Out of about a gazillion people, this made her pretty special.

So anyway I told her this, and because I have amazing manners I suggested we don't talk about Ex-Girlfriend-Not-Girlfriend because it'd be sort of unethical, seeing as my end of that conversation has words in it like '*She cheated on me!*', and '*She broke mah little heart!*', and then some. Inappropriate stuff to tell a mutual friend. Self-restraint! Halo intact! Also I asked her not to mention me to Ex-G-Not-G, so that we could be friends in private and I wouldn't have to think about Ex-G-Not-G being on the periphery of my life in any way. Because I can't be bothered thinking about her. And the poison that comes with it. No big deal, but still. I do like my privacy.

Then about a month ago New-ish Friend told me she remembered having dinner with me. We were on the train home and she brought up the Ex-Girlfriend-Not-Girlfriend subject. Told me Ex-G-Not-G had been mean to other people, a good place to start a snowball on the topic. She told me that at this dinner Ex-G-Not-G had made a subtly unkind comment to me about my kids and the schooling options I was considering. I didn't remember the dinner, and I didn't remember the barbed comment. But it sounded very Ex-G-Not-G-ish.

Despite that, I thought New-ish Friend had me confused with somebody else. But then yesterday she sent me a text that ended with '*...you have a gorgy week x*'. And suddenly I remembered. That was *her*? I clearly remember writing an entry about people who say "gorgy". Which was, at the time, one of those flouncy rich-isms I always came across when going out with Ex-Girlfriend-Not-Girlfriend, the rich-isms that made me feel like all of her people were from another planet.

Is it possible that I was mean to my new-ish friend? In my deep dark past? I don't think I was mean because I remember liking Gorgy Woman. But now I'm scared; I'm going to have to rummage through my old blog entries to find it before I see her next, and then I'm going to have to tell her about it, and to apologise for my maybe-meanness, because it'd be wrong not to disclose something like that.

Me and my big mouth. Me and my stupid honesty. It's kinda funny, but I hope she has a forgiving temperament.

p.s. The funny thing is, this friend is the only person I know who can say the word "gorgy" and get away with it. It suits her perfectly. She makes it sound natural. Who'da thought that was even possible?

———

Monday, 17th September, 2012.

Out With the Old, In With the New

First-Born ditched The Bigot. I didn't write about that because I felt guilty for not liking them enough, and it happened within days of my writing that bogan entry.

And I know it's not good to introduce First-Born's New Partner in the same entry as I get rid of the old one, but housework is housework and it has to be done. So – I'm announcing the acquisition of First-Born's New Partner because this one's the keeper. This one's so beautiful I'm already planning the wedding and addressing them as Child-in-Law. Is so beautiful, in fact, that I might just shorten that to My Child. Eventually. When I get to know them better and it's not likely to scare them off.

Anyway, First-Born's New Partner has a Kombi [!!], which they park at the top of my driveway. I always wanted a Kombi parked at the top of my driveway; it's one of those things you don't realise you always wanted until you get it.

AND, one of the first things they did was ask my permission to "see" my child. This is particularly hilarious. Especially in their thick Yorkshire accent.

AND, First-Born was eager for me to get home because they wanted me to meet New Partner and give my approval, in that way we do when we read somebody and say to each other *'They're okay'*. The point being that my opinion matters to First-Born in a big fat way. Which is really, really nice.

ALSO, New Partner plays the piano IN MY HOUSE. AND, you should see how happy First-Born is.

And the last AND is that you should see us, hanging around in the kitchen having conversations. We're not just normal now, we're so normal we're practically Super Normal. I still have to pinch myself to believe it's real. If you saw us you'd never believe that those seven years happened. (Seven and a half, but who's counting.)

I love that when I finally get my family back, it kinda grows a little, so that with Son's Girlfriend and First-Born's New Partner I now have more kids than I started with. [Normal!!]

p.s. As I write this, New Partner's upstairs playing the piano. I need to get cleaning fluid from the laundry so that I can clean my bathroom, because I'm going to my nephew's wedding tonight and I can't go to a wedding with a dirty bathroom. But I don't want to push past New Partner because they might stop. What to do?

That's my small family. I also have my big family on my mind. Nephew's wedding. This is just a count your blessings thing – I have a great family.

Thursday, 27th September, 2012.

Eureka!

October's looking good because I've discovered the library. I know they've existed for a very long time, libraries, but it didn't occur to me that they'd be good for something other than the storing and borrowing of books.

So there I was with somebody's thesis in my hands, and I wandered behind the bookshelves to see what was there, and discovered a big study area with desks by a long window. When I sat down there to read it occurred to me that it was pretty fucking peaceful.

The peace was shocking, especially for an essentially quiet person who can't find the stuff anywhere.

Who'da thought? But anyway, even though the air conditioning made me dizzy and I really wanted to open that nice window to get some fresh air, it felt good enough sitting there to be able to write. So I've hatched a plan to defeat the impossibility of working at home: come to skool every day, spend three hours in the library with my lap top WRITING MY NOVEL, and then a few hours in the studio.

Why I didn't think of this before I don't know, but I'm so excited I'm practically hyperventilating. A whole space there just for writing, and a solution to the year's big problem. I feel like I've discovered gold.

Saturday, 29th September, 2012

Animal Den

I was listening to a podcast about crime scene cleaners in America recently, and when asked what it's like to be confronted by the gruesomeness of brutal deaths the cleaning person said that once you get used to it it's not the way people die that's shocking, but seeing the way people live. Because most people are filthy. He hadn't realised how dirty people can be. *And that*, he said, *is the depressing part of the job*.

I had to nod my head in agreement because we are those people, we live in that house. Especially now, because Mother is on strike again. Mother wants her children to show they care by cleaning the fuck up.

It's not gonna happen. My beggary's going unrewarded, and my appeals to their consciences to make the last few weeks of my course do-able are being ignored.

It's depressing, the man was right. You only need to raise uncooperative teenagers to see how much dirt a single human can generate.

So I'm not getting much sleep, I don't get to use my time the way I want to, and I can't keep on top of my offsprings' filth without giving even more of my time and my headspace away, first on the task and then on the resentment.

I hope nobody murders us, because if a crime scene cleaner comes in and takes our lives by surprise, they're gonna get really depressed.

October 2012

Monday, 1st October, 2012.

Day One Down

There's a reason they use sleep deprivation as a form of torture. More beggary on my part, but it's no use. Instead of getting better, or even staying the same, the situation's gotten much worse. I'm getting so little sleep I can't even drive my car without going into a weird trance, blurring my vision to cope with the fact that my eyes are open.

First-Born's gone from being a partially considerate nocturnal creature, to a noisy inconsiderate nocturnal creature. To cope with this I stay in bed for between ten and twelve hours, trying to make up for the sleep I lose, but in the end for those ten or so hours I only get between three and five hours of sleep. More often three than five.

This morning, after a really bad night, I decided to stay in bed and wait for sleepiness to hit me, because I'm just so tired, and started to doze off at around 7:30. At 7:45 the property two doors up started running machinery.

This was like no machinery I've ever heard before; the sound came through in waves that vibrated through solid objects. I tried to cover my ears but it made no difference, it was like something from a sci-fi movie that pulses through your body and makes your internal organs explode. My ribcage felt so fragile, my nerves in pure distress. And it stopped and started in bastard intervals, revving up from a slow start until the world was screaming, and then cutting off every ten minutes. Over and over again, for hours. I was in tears, and imagined everybody on the hillside with hands clamped over their ears, crying out in agony.

I wished that somebody who'd had sleep would be thoughtful enough to call the police. Or to walk over to that motherfucker and stab him [gently?]. Yes, I really thought that. Maybe I'm not as mild mannered as I thought.

So anyway, this is it. This is October. Instead of being up at 6 am for a fruitful day of Octobery bounty, I'm up at 11, needing to dump these thoughts, because how on earth am I going to write fiction with this disappointment in my head, and this panic, and desperation?

I'm so upset. This was going to be the symbolic month in which I actively take back control of my life. I can't even begin to describe what it means, symbolically, to have that opportunity ruined. I don't know how to save today. Or how to save the month.

Can we just start October tomorrow? What am I going to do???

Saturday, 6th October, 2012.

Begging, So Badly

For sleep. All week, so little of the stuff. Three hours a night, sometimes a bit more. So when First-Born and New Partner went out for the night, I went to bed early.

Couldn't believe it when I heard/felt my phone vibrate one hour later. Text from First-Born's New Partner. Said *hi how ya goin.* Then one saying *Get outa bed plze,* which is just creepy. And I thought, if this is deliberate, to wake me as a joke because they think it's funny that I've had no sleep (I've been begging and begging, every day, for them to let me sleep), they'll do this every hour. Then one hour later, New Partner rang me. Started a friendly conversation. Pissed as a fart. I was so confused.

Went upstairs to Son, in tears, and he rang them. Turns out it was a silly joke = NP was trying to chat me up to be funny. Apparently *Get outa bed plz* is a bootie call. (So illogical.)

First-Born was angry at New Partner because they didn't know NP was doing it. Funny mofo. And yet, so not funny. So Son sent First-Born a text for me, basically *stop being a colossal cunt basket... out of line, let mum sleep* et cetera, and called them. No, I can't imagine Son ever using the C word either, and am appropriately impressed.

Awake 'til 2;30 ish, slept 'til 8:30, then 9-9;30ish. A dream = as small creatures we took a wrong turn in a mindscape; thought *need that road fixed* but = First-Born and I plummeted = I grabbed them and made sure I'd land first to hopefully soften their fall = I'd die for them, or already had given up life for them? = held them close and kissed their cheek saying '*I love you*', then I prepared to die.

Waking = pain = like somebody had stuck a crow bar into my middle and stirred up my meat. Wondered if heart okay, could feel it beat, but then remembered visiting physio. Girly push-ups caused the pain? Anyway, not used to feeling my inner meats like that, tearing from their lodgings.

Monday, 8th October, 2012.

Well That's That Then

First-Born's New Partner isn't my future child-in-law anymore. The gloss has worn off because of they woke me, and because they thought I was schizo for losing my nut one night (well, First-Born and I do have a history, so I'm allowed to lose my nut). New Partner should just grow some balls. If they can't handle that, they can't handle First-Born.

Plus the Kombi's broken, as they do, and once you've seen somebody without their Kombi you're seeing them for who they really are.

They won't last. First-Born usually leaves them after I stop thinking they're okay for them, even though they don't know I've stopped thinking they're okay. Good.

Saturday, 13th October, 2012.

Lap Lane Rage

When you're at the pool it's clear that humans are just animals who like to gather at the waterhole. We hang around in the shallows spraying water over our backs with our trunks, while waterbirds build their nests on the shore.

That is, it's supposed to be a pleasant, social experience. So I'm not proud of this, and have probably confessed to this before. I swim to relax, and to stretch, and for the bliss, but my usually mild-mannered self is transformed by other people's bad etiquette in the lap lanes. I took out a local membership so that I could swim every day, which I do, and it's getting harder and harder to find the pool peaceful.

It's not just the elderlies, but you know, they do suck. Now, I work with elderly people and like interacting with "them", but you get me into that pool and I'm utterly age-ist. If I end up in the lane next to the people doing their aqua-aerobics I practically gag at the smell of unwashed hair and the thought of their antiquarian skin cells falling off into the water.

Why they don't put their heads under the water is beyond me – why would you not put your head underwater? How could you possibly feel refreshed with a submerged body and dry head? But anyway, the smelly heads, and smelly old-lady face powder. Letting their floaty boards and their polystyrene noodles drift into my lane. (Those things have been between their legs!!) And then today, a doddering old man got into my lane just as I was approaching the end of a lap and started WALKING right where I was about to swim. Plus I could smell his toothpaste. Selfish old cnuts, the lot of 'em.

The non-elderlies = slower people go in front of you without asking you if you want to go first; faster ones hop into your lane and use flippers so that you can't properly align your speed to keep out of their way, and so on. There's more, but I won't list everything. I'm sick of being one of the only few who have manners.

So my peaceful demeanour changes. I don't like to stop, so if I have to stop at the end of a lap I say *'Oh fuck'* and half-stand because I can't just keep going. Actually, I don't really, I put the *oh* there to make it sound softer. I just say *fuck,* outright. Sometimes *fucken hell.* Nobody can hear me, they're swimming, but I kinda hope the CCTV observers are lip reading so that they can take the hint and give us more lanes. Three to a lane is two too many. What they're really probably thinking is *'Watch this one, she could get nasty'*, and prepping a team to escort me from the venue.

So there ya go. Temper tantrum. I just want my peace. Is that too much to ask? Old people. *Pffft.*

Anonymosity

Monday, 15th October, 2012.

Mnph

My eyeballs hurt by morning, because I only got 1.5 hours of sleep. As mentioned before, the way it works with First-Born banging about the house all night like a ghost with good intentions but clunky feet, is that when it's bad I have to stay in bed for 12 hours to get between three and five hours' sleep. Most of it waiting. Last night I was in bed for seven hours and got 1.5.

I'd been up late working on a drawing, and they woke me up at 3:45 am. I tried to get back to sleep but couldn't; then they went out at 6:30 am. Me: wide awake.

1.5 hours. This why I have to sit down and write about it. Sheer incredulity.

So I dragged myself out of bed for a swim, and it was the nicest swim. I know this is hyperbole, but nothing's as nice as being in the water. Even when I'm exhausted.

Anyway, I'm sad about today because I missed the last class presentations, because it wouldn't have been safe for me to drive in to the studios. It's like missing a movie that only plays once in a lifetime and is then destroyed.

The only bright side is that it means more time to spend on my drawing; the two-day drawing that's taking me four days to finish. I'm crawling all over the floor to reach its parts. It's big and solid and graceless and if it's daggy I don't care. Time I owned my dagginess. If I'm not fit to put things into the world yet then I never will be; this is pretty much what I have in me.

I'm so tired I can't even write a whole sentence. Much.

Tuesday, 16th October, 2012.

Noise

I sat here to say something but I can't remember what it was. So let's just count the sleep hours. Under five last night, because I worked late in the studio and then First-Born woke me up by knocking at the front door at 5:17 am, having forgotten their key. Kind of waltzes in as though that's okay.

Now they're doing the dishes, which is point scoring, except that when I said '*Can you please turn that off?*' to their music, on accounta I'm dog tired and ready to sleep, or collapse, they replied with '*Can you just leave*', in that tone they reserve especially for me.

And now I'm all weepy, which is weird because I hardly ever cry anymore. Kind of spent my capacity for tears on those bastard years. Just so tired, is the thing. And my body aching and my future ridiculous because I have no dag-filter so the drawing I've loved doing for four days and nights straight is now looking really stupid, as everything does when I realise I have to show it to people. Not my favourite thing, being public.

So, the aching. It's not just that I don't get sleep, it's that I can't imagine sleep ever being possible. First-Born's more work than a newborn.

Summary:
Every day is pot luck. I can't plan anything because I don't know when and for how long they're going to keep me awake. Didn't go in to the skool studios yesterday as I wanted to, nor today. Too tired. This situation's unworkable. Nah duh. How the hell am I going to fix it. QUESTION MARK.

Saturday, 27th October, 2012.

The Elves and the Shoe Maker
I was an elf, working secretly through the night to make something for somebody not to help them out of necessity, but out of love, although it was for a teacher so it's not really love, more like an affectionate respect.

I did this even though the sleep count for the nights preceding Thursday night had been five, four and zero (the zero being restful wakefulness with intermittent dozing, which is better than nothing).

Anonymosity

So in order to get to work by 6:30 am, I got three hours' sleep. Because I also had to finish my Honours application. [BUSY.]

I think now that elves generally get a rough deal. Because here's what happened: we chose the teacher we wanted to buy for from a list, and teamed up to make/buy presents to give to them at our art department party, that being the tradition.

There were three (and then four) people in my team, and when we met to discuss the present the Male Member [!] was very pushy, making the decision for us like a patriarchal father who won't be reasoned with. He said that we should buy her a bottle of wine and some flowers and that's it, meaning that he didn't want to make any effort whatsoever. He even said *'I've already paid my fees, they're just doing their job, why should I have to give them more than that...'*, and so on. Very domineering, and our suggestions were quickly dismissed.

So when he waved his share of the money around and asked *'Who wants to do the shopping?'* I said *ME!* knowing that I could then shove his flowers idea and get her something more interesting.

I thought of making a crown because the teacher is acting Head of Skool, and asked Ace Young Friend for advice. She also said *'Maybe a crown?'* for the same reason, and seeing as we had matching light bulbs going off above our heads I figured it must be a good idea. So I called Other Present Friend and said let's-go-behind-his-back and asked her to make the crown, while I make a sceptre. The plan was to present it to the teacher on a red cushion.

When we were at the party and I said I wasn't sure about getting up in front of everyone to give it to her, Male Member [!!] said *'I'll do it'* and took the pieces from our hands. I actually let him, even though I didn't want to. Because here he was riding in on his muscular steed to take the credit for the love and sleeplessness that went into preparing the present. It was like having your macaroni pasting stolen by the bully at kindergarten.

Except it was my own fault. I'm not nervous about getting up in front of people, so I can only put it down to persistent sleeplessness that I felt so unsure and crowd-shy.

Anyway it was nice. Everybody cheered as Male Member [!!] knelt down to present the gift and Other Present Friend put the crown on

Teacher's head. Other Other Present Friend gave her the bottle of wine, and all the chocolates fell out. It was a really happy moment, and I was kind of shocked that I'd made it happen but wasn't part of it.

Seriously, why did I do that? My fault, but I'm still pissed off. Possibly with myself more than with Male Member [!!]. Fucking *men*, though. When The Teacher placed her hand on his shoulder as she passed by and he accepted the affection as though he'd actually been thoughtful, I wanted to puke at the insincerity.

Guh. The lesson for today, children, is that you shouldn't be such a pussy, and that if you're gonna work so hard to make sure your teacher feels the student-love in the room, then you should be in there delivering it.

Also, elves are dumb, because anonymous giving is pooh. Consider the lesson learned.

———

November 2012

Saturday, 17th November, 2012.

Remembering how to stop and think out loud.
A kick in the teeth that he'd [hypothetically] rather live with First-Born, when they caused so much hardship and difficulty, than with me, who he says is easy to live with.

Wednesday, 21st November, 2012.

InValid-ictory
Don't mind me, I'm just preparing for the oncoming empty-nest syndrome. So emotional I can't stand it, what with Son telling me he's going to leave home before I'm ready.

And tonight, dropping him at his valedictory dinner, driving in to the car park and seeing so many cars, all of which belong to people who are loved by their children. Children who do things like go WITH THEIR PARENTS to valedictory dinners.

One day I'll write more about this, but for now I'm just touching upon something significant. Because it's such a sad thing, and I have to find a way to show him that it's his inadequacy, not mine. I may have failed at Family, but I had help.

I thought I was doing the right thing, giving him space. Apparently I gave him too much.

Sunday, 25th November, 2012.

Pre
Operation Secret Friendship: underway. Rendezvous: today.

Allegedly, according to mutual acquaintances, I'm supposed to hate this man sooner or later, so if I'm going to have an affair with him

I have to do it before that happens. Probably a stupid thing to do. The variables of how he behaves afterwards – the great unknown.

I can't fall in love with him. There's no one I can fall in love with yet. Those people live under rocks and are difficult to bump into.

So this man. He'll do. Even though I'll regret it afterwards. My body's made the decision for me. (Anybody will do!) (As long as they smell nice. And he does.)

Still Sunday, 25th November, 2012.

Addendum

No, I can't go through with it. He wore socks with his shorts and dresses like a seventy year-old. I've reformed a socially awkward man before, and can't go through that again. You give them youth by association but eventually their instinctive old-mannishness trumps all of your hard work.

And yet... when we were lying inside an art thing together he rolled over and I saw the bulk of his package (I know it's crass, but that word makes me laugh) and it set me off all over again.

What's a nice girl like me doing looking at packages?

I need another human being, that's the problem. Nobody ever stops needing another human being, really, but I need one NOW and YESTERDAY and it's making me contemplate doing the very stupid. Because he's convenient, and it's so secret, and because I'm stronger than him. And because I can.

Perhaps if I keep the lights off.

You see? There's a solution to every problem. So did I just talk myself back into it? (Really, that desperate?)

Operation Secret Friendship: established. What happens next, who knows.

Thursday, 29th November, 2012.

Purple

That's the colour of his prose, I'm sorry to say. If you want a love affair with somebody like me you have to be as not-purple as it's possible to be. But there it is, in my in-box. An e-mail describing a romantic scenario based on an experience we had when looking at art, and it's so purple it's bruised.

And overtly sexual.

When I opened that e I was kinda shocked at how direct he was being. And let the record state that I haven't flirted with him – not one little bit. I've just been friendly, as I am with everybody. No gestures, no suggestive looks, no ambiguous words. Just happy conversation, all very careful.

Maybe I'm giving off pheromones I don't know about? Sending them out to any old body?

Anyway that was yesterday – I read the e and went into panic mode, with no idea of how to handle the situation. It took me hours to come up with a solution, that being to reply to his email with a counter-romantic scenario. First I wrote one that was brutal, and then I softened it and just made it realistic, making his characters grate on each other in a tired, old married way. And then I closed the e-mail with '*Reality is a bad habit of mine*'.

I felt so clever. Undoing the romance so bluntly shoulda been enough to convey the message that the romance isn't going to happen. It was supposed to convey that message without hurting his feelings. I like him – I don't want to hurt him. It's silly to have known somebody for such a short amount of time and even be ABLE to hurt them.

But when I checked e-mails after my swim this morning, there he was. I read it and said '*Oh nooooo*' out loud, because this time I'm really in trouble. He countered my counter-romance by having the man be considerate inside my alternative scenario. He calls them lovers, inside these scenarios, and includes a lot of kissing and physical and emotional *fulfillment*. It's just crazy that he had the man undo his arseholeness. You can't undo arseholeness like that – once it's happened the marriage is over.

Anyway, he's very sweet, and he's trying to display his sweetness in this e-mail the same way he was trying to display his sensuality in the last one. But the worst of it is that he sent a p.s. today, and that p.s. said '*She looked fantastic on the other side of that... [I'm censoring where we were]*'.

That's a very direct compliment. I have to answer that, and I have no idea how. I have to have "the conversation" with him. How's he even being so forward? I'd understand it if we'd been on a date or something.

Anyway. I'll have to make him think I'm a pure lesbian. A soiled one, granted, but pure nonetheless. It'll require socialising with him, which is okay. I'm happy to be friends. But oh lawdy, what a painful little bit of socialising this is gonna be.

Friday, 30th November, 2012.

It Gets Worse

This is why people have casual sex. I've just worked that out. Because it's okay if they pull you aside and bend you over a chair to politely frick you legless before you know a thing about them, but it's not okay for them to email you with sappy fantasies that reveal far too much about the innards of their brains.

I know far too much about the innards of his brain. And now he's asked me out. By email. In third person. What has she to say about this, I don't know. She doesn't quite know what to do.

I confess I have a deep fear of him wearing socks with his shorts again. And I now know how he interprets my friendliness very specifically. Because he told me, in third person, how my face lit up when I saw him. [Allegedly.] For the record, my face lights up when I see anybody.

Yesterday, when he was around, I was thinking that I don't mind him in person. In fact I like him being around in that singular context. But I don't want other contexts. I also realised that I make him laugh a lot, but he doesn't make me laugh at all. In fact, he makes me anti-laugh. This seems to be more important than I realised – that somebody making you laugh is inevitable when your wits are matched. And when somebody can surprise you with what they say, or add something new to your mind. People do that to each other all the time.

I need an equal. Even my casual sex has to be equal. Which is why I'm no good at it. And which really sucks, because I can't fall in love.

My poor body. If I could just sever it from my mind I'd have a much funner life.

Still Friday, 30th November, 2012.

Best Rejection Line Ever

Sorry, I can't go on a date with you because I need to stay home and write a book.

That's also the gosh-honest truth. First of December tomorrow, and firsts are good for resuming work on novels. What decent man wouldn't be okay with honesty like that?

December 2012

Saturday, 1st December, 2012.

You know how you get home from work and lie down on the floor for a think because you're going to a party in the city but the idea of it isn't very appealing because even though it's a really good friend's 30th and you haven't seen her for so long, you start to worry that it'll be too noisy to talk to anybody and you're going by yourself and that just reminds you that no matter how many friends you have you're still lonely, so you keep lying on the floor but then you get up and have a shower n' get dressed up in the prettiest dress and you look like you should be at a party even if you don't feel like it, but you're still thinking about how it might be horrible because it's such a long way and you love seeing her friends because they all work in libraries n wot not but they're all also much younger and full of youthful enthusiasm that you just can't feel and the idea of having to socialise awkwardly over loud music is awful and yet what if you meet somebody nice but really when do you ever meet somebody really nice that you can actually become friends with afterwards when you go to these things (the answer is never) so you piss fart around and then three hours pass and it's so late because your prodigal friend has called you for a chat and then you get into the car and start driving and you know you really should be at a party in that dress because your body feels lovely but still you're not sure of the emotional investment in conversations that are nice at the time but lead to more loneliness and it's such a long way, so you pull the car over three times and then keep going, telling yourself *I'll get petrol and then make up my mind* and you get petrol and then keep going but suddenly, without even thinking further, you turn around to go home and you stop at Safeway to get cat biscuits and chocolate and then you get home and REGRET it because you love your friend and really think you need to be at that party no matter how far away and lonely it is?

Sucks. I suck. Tomorrow, novel writing resumption Day Two. I have to shake this icky I-didn't-go-to-the-party feeling before morning.

I've effectively just spent four hours actively not-going to a party I wanted to go to. In that time I could have gone and stayed and then come all the way back. I'm such a bad friend. But really, I'm so mentally tired, and quietly in writer-mode. And, yes, tired of doing things alone.

I knew I'd feel this bad if I turned around. Nobody in a dress this pretty should feel bad. If only I didn't over-think every single damn fucking thing.

Sunday, 2nd December, 2012. 12:45am

Two Bads in One Night

Sitting here in my very pretty dress, regretting not being at that party like you wouldn't believe, I've just written the let's-be-friends e-mail (as opposed to let's-be-lovers) to The Little Man (that's what the girls call him, because of his stature), and I feel mean to have sent something so blunt, even though it's not that blunt, still friendly, but blunt enough seeing as it says *no way not in a million years*.

He's built a very elaborate fantasy up around me, the details of which I unfortunately know. But even if he hadn't, no matter how you write something like that, it's going to make the recipient sad. Something else to have to clear from my mind before I resume writing in the morning.

I do life so stupidly. I hope this doesn't make it hard to sleep.

Sunday, 2nd December, 2012.

When Bad Turns to Awful: One

This is a rap over the knuckles because it's so much more than bad, not to have gone to that party. I'm so selfish. Stupid for assuming I'm not important enough to not have been missed, for one thing. As though I'm part of a past that doesn't matter anymore. But selfish more than anything.

What I've done is confused two worlds. With most of my art people I'm a very social introvert who survives a very extroverted world. So many friends, but I connect with only a few of them on a deeper level. And when we socialise in groups I do sometimes wish I wasn't there, because everything's so much on the surface it doesn't feel real, and when you go home alone it really is lonely. Like you've spent yourself on nothing, even though there's plenty of love to go around.

But this friend, she's not art world. She's literary world. I don't label my people, but there's a huge difference. We connect all the way. That we're apart now is my fault, for being old, busy, broken and overwhelmed by all of that extrovertedness. I thought I was over that.

I felt good last night. I would have gone there feeling good and even if I'd felt like an outsider, seeing my friend on a drunken in her happy life would've been a beautiful thing. Our mutual friend wasn't there because they don't see each other any more, but it wouldn't have mattered. We'd have hugged and rekindled our friend-love, which I miss like crazy today, and all would have been peachy.

One art friend = texting to invite herself for a sleepover next weekend, and within an hour another one asking me to visit again soon = I've found the most beautiful people. I'm so glad school's over, and all of the shallow running around. I'm allowed to slow down, and be a real friend again. I should've started with that party, despite the crowd.

So today I'm grinding this lesson into my brain: this invisible loneliness is a fiction and I have to not think about it. My impulse was to go to the party and I should have followed it through. Like I almost did. Thinking I don't matter is a residue of those horrible parenting years, and I have to get over it. Which also confuses me, because I thought I had. I'm outrageously happy. Not this minute, because I'm such a scum-sucking cretin of a friend, but generally.

I don't know how to undo this kind of thing. Except to love my friend properly, ASAP.

When Bad Turns to Awful: Two

Ohhhh, awful doesn't begin to describe it. My e-mail told him no, very directly. I was so frank I may have to change my name.

But this morning, two more emails from him. It's not nice to quote something so personal, but this is anonymous, so maybe it's okay? I don't want to violate his privacy. Which I kind of already have.

He's said he'll find another job if it means he'll be allowed to date me. He says: '*It is rare to find a more [inteleigent] beautiful and warm woman as you*'. (That's a cut and paste – his spelling, not mine. Plus no contractions; you won't find me writing without contractions.) (Or commas. You can do without them, but not always.)

He says: '*I will see you tomorrow darling, my [hart] and spirit wait in anticipation*'.

He says in his p.s. that we could go slow, and that I'm '*the beautiful light and warmth that I have been looking for*'.

I'm so naive, for not realising that saying hello to people means "let's fuck" these days. Or worse, that being friendly means "let's fall in love".

In my other worlds you can be friends with everybody and nobody misinterprets what you say or do. Girls are allowed to be friends with boys and we don't even catch germs from each other. When we hug each other we don't even fall pregnant.

This is the 21st century, isn't it?

This is so messy. I can't be mean to him, but is that what I have to do? Or will the lesbian card work? It's just so silly to have to lie. I don't mind dishonesty when it's necessary, but really, I don't like being forced into it. Like I need that kind of encouragement.

Maybe it's the bad karma I deserve for not going to parties. The right people aren't going to fall in love with you if you don't go out and get down n' jiggy with 'em. From that perspective, the wrong people are my just desserts.

Thursday, 6th December, 2012.

WhoreMoans

Forgive the title. Another secret man, this one also smitten, this one also a bad speller, so bad I had to tell him to restrict our conversations to in-person only because his spelling was making me sick.

Yesterday I woke with so many love bites on my neck I had to buy foundation on the way to work to cover them before I went in. (I have to wear my hair up.) Possibly the most satisfying neck-kissing I've ever experienced, please forgive the hyperbole.

So although I think it's hilarious that I called somebody and said *'Tonight, just once, let's,'* it's not so hilarious that I have this memory of that neck kissing, and that tomorrow night I'll be calling him to say *'Again, just once more'*.

Because I'm aware, this time, of how much power I'm exercising over another human being. I shouldn't be loving it, but I am. I've had to be brutally mean to him to keep him in check and I shouldn't be loving that either, but I do.

The sad thing is I don't even like his penis, I just loved having the damn thing inside me. This is the first time I've ever been able to enjoy sex without emotion, I think? I have no idea what's gotten into me (besides the obvious). Usually I'm at least good friends with my partners. Is this just fast-tracking my way through a desperate need for intimacy? Is it all of the sudden freedom, finally? A bit of reckless abandon?

On another note, secrets are erotic things. Except that you can't talk to anybody about them. And they require wearing make up on your neck.

Enough, I need sleep. It's bad enough to be acting like a teenager, let alone to be writing about it. Speaking of which, I'm writing well in the mornings. Maybe getting this out of my system is necessary. For however long it takes.

Saturday, 15th December, 2012.

The Plot Thickens

Apparently I've been dating a woman. She's very beautiful, this woman, but I didn't realise I was dating her until we were sitting in a cinema and the movie's homo-erotic scene came on. She giggled and held my hand. I experienced two reactions at that point; the first was panic, my mind quickly racing over the events of our short acquaintance to try to determine exactly how this moment had happened. The second was overwhelming sexual arousal, because as we're beginning to establish, I'm turning into a bit of a slut.

I didn't kiss her in the cinema. I knew she wanted me to, but I kept watching the movie as she stroked my hair. I caressed her hand, but it was crowded and the nearby people were already annoyed by her frequent talking, so I kept it clean. And also kept on panicking. Because I knew then as I know now, I can't love her. I knew that soon I'd have to hurt her. I haven't hurt her yet, but you know, I'm gonna.

The facts: I work with her; she's from Thailand and has reasonably good/very poor English; is studying now and has studied before; came to Australia for another woman who I suspect didn't treat her very well; she has life experience that's so different from mine it'd be impossible for me to fall in proper love with her. Plus the language barrier = it's incredibly hard work talking to her, and intellectual complexity's out of the question. I am, how you say, frustrated.

I thought the dates were friendship. Didn't know she's homosexual. Didn't even suspect she's homosexual. I thought the chocolates and the other [outrageously generous] presents were a cultural thing (like the Japanese). The gazillion texts she's been sending me each day should have tipped me off. The demands for me to reply to those texts more frequently than I do should also have tipped me off. That she wore make-up when she saw me could possibly have tipped me off. When we met for coffee I watched her talk to me and thought of her as a gorgeous little creature; I really do think she's beautiful. I love working with her, but anyway, the coffee, the phone calls, the dinner and the movie, all paid for by her... and then after the movie walking me to my car. A very hasty possibly-nervous kiss, too fast for me to feel sensual, but mechanically okay. Just, with me still processing how I'd somehow led her on without realising, it was kind of a shock.

And as she drove off, I said '*Oh no*' out loud again, over and over. Because really. *Fuck.*

I've said already I'm in an alternative universe, only this time my asking her to dance at the staff Xmas party seems to have been mistaken for a wedding proposal. She didn't dance with me, by the way. I've since found out that she was worried our colleagues would realise what was happening. Which is really funny, because even I didn't realise what was happening. Instead she sent me texts telling me that when I danced I was *'cheeky and sexy'*, but I think she meant it as a thing that frightened her.

The way she interprets the most innocent things as significant is driving me crazy.

So, more. Other alleged dates. I finally had "the talk" with her, and again I lied, this time about my ex-husband coming to Melbourne soon to win me back. (I have his permission for this lie. He's proving very useful.)

I felt so mean. I also don't think she fully understood. So when I took her to the movies again, this time me paying, and we again held hands, it was okay because my plan was to let her down gently, by showing her first how beautiful she is. Back in the car afterwards there was a lot of kissing, more than kissing, and we could have had sex then and there. She asked *'Can we go somewhere'* and I said yes, but then I just took her home. I couldn't go through with it. Kinda felt wrong? No emotional investment on my part, and her investing so much.

It's so bizarre, and I'm slightly pissed off, because I didn't ask for this. I think she should have asked my permission first, instead of just presuming. So now I'm responsible for somebody against my will. And she calls and calls and calls. I talk to her while I'm out walking, which means I'm getting no private think-time. The worst thing is our work friendship was perfect, and I didn't want it to change.

So. I'm heartless and my headspace is being eaten alive by things I don't want to have to deal with. And because I'm having outrageously good and frequent sex with a man at the moment, I'm cheating on a girlfriend who isn't even my girlfriend. I am, accidentally, *somebody's girlfriend*. Weird.

Monday, 17th December, 2012.

...and thickens some more

Now let's talk about him. But first let's establish that I'm no goddess, so I don't quite know why these people are all falling for me. I'm always happy, I guess. That could be attractive. And I do love everybody, so I kinda throw the more innocent version of that emotion around quite a lot. And I have woken up from a long sort of coma, so I'm very energised and bursting out of my own skin. Perhaps these things, I don't know? I'm either doing something very right or something very wrong, and am too naive to know what it is. It's best to think of it as a temporary blip in the status quo.

(The elderly people at work – who I *love* – call me "Sunny". The funny thing about that is that the ones who can't remember my actual name do remember to call me that, which amounts to the same mental process, so why they can remember one and not the other is beyond me.) (The ones who do remember my name say it aloud, over and over. There's one table of men who, when I'm serving their meals, love to sing my name out almost-together, '*Chris-Chris-Chris-Chris-Chris*', so that when I approach they sound like a nest full of chirping baby birds. It's very cute.)

But anyway. Him.

Despite having made an accidental marriage proposal to my alleged-girlfriend at the work Xmas party, when I finally left I sat in the car quite aware that I was in no state to drive, and I called him. The man, forgive the details, can go for hours. And my body = still insatiable = pure liquid = very, very satisfying sex. Too satisfying. I've gone for so long without and now I can't stand the idea of going without for very long at all.

And in the middle of it all I just hold my breath and wonder how I'm allowed to feel this good.

The poor man is behaving himself and obeys my rules, but I know he's in love. This makes me feel both good and bad. I'm human, see. And it was really nice that the next time I called him, when I insisted we stay in the car because it's a no-man's land, between places, he turned his car into a cubby so that it was like a little house, seats collapsed and mattress in the back, with wine and a picnic and everything. Turns out he's able to surprise me pleasantly.

But no love. I can't. I just don't. It's all about the hunger for me. I bite him a lot. He turns up to work with hickeys all over his neck and teeth marks on his shoulders. We're both battered n' bruised and walking around tenderly with our pulled muscles. Breaststroke in the pool has become a real challenge for my thighs.

So how and where does it end ???

I see him way too often. I have to proceed carefully. The other day he started a sentence with '*When you dump me...*' and I told him that he won't be dumped, that we'll transition to friendship. But he mostly speaks about our future as though I'm going to fall for him, too, and I know I'm not. For one thing it would've happened by now. There's just not enough I can share with him.

I was at a picnic recently, sitting next to a man I've known for a couple of years, a friend-to-be who I haven't gone all the way in establishing a friendship with yet. He's a funny-lookin' thing, and I have a quiet curiosity about him. It's possible I like him. He turns up whenever I'm talking to other people in our group, but I don't know if that's because of me or just coincidence. In any case, that's the kind of pre-attraction I like, because it happens so gently. Just curiosity. Maybe I like you, that sort of thing. In the process of finding out.

I won't see him for at least a month, and wish I'd spoken to him more when I saw him.

Doesn't matter. Just, it's nice to know these things that are happening with people I'm so emotionally detached from won't go on forever, and that there's something different in the future. Something nicer and more mutual. If I'm lucky.

Sigh. Write a damn book, you. I'm supposed to be concentrating on my work. I am, but not as much as I need to. How people who do this sort of thing all the time and still manage to get any work done, I don't know. Other people's emotions are exhausting.

Thursday, 20th December, 2012.

Sweet Nothings

I had the girl problem sorted, I thought. Pushed back to a comfortable shade of friendship. We went walking. She came to my home and I dragged her around my hillside in the dark. We hugged goodbye at the top of my driveway, but that's all. I was SO relieved.

Then after she'd gone I went to meet up with The Man (just to prove that I have no scruples).

Next night, after we finished our shift together at work, we did the Thousand Steps. We came back to my house first, and after I'd changed into walking clothes she cornered me in my bedroom doorway to tell me she can't lie to me, because she thinks I'm very *'hot and sexy'*, and she can't help herself because I'm *'so attract'* [broken English]. I knew this because I kept catching her looking my body up and down at work. Kinda creepy, if you must know. Not very subtle at all.

Anyway, then she kissed me. There in the doorway to my bedroom. Fast kissing again, and all my fault because in order to establish the friendship so that she knew I was genuine about it, I'd invited her to lunch a few days before. She kissed me in the car before she went to work that day. I liked it that time, even though it was still fast. I think I liked it because it couldn't go anywhere, and I *love* kissing.

Back to my doorway. I stopped her by saying *'We'd better get going for that walk'*. I was disappointed because I knew that the walk wasn't really just a walk with a friend anymore. I was gonna have to deal with this again.

I forgot what a rush it is to climb that hill. I also forgot how quick it is, which is disappointing. I had to stop to wait for her to catch up a few times, but she was okay. And the downhill slope's a bummer because it hurts my knees. I wish I could find a hill like that that just keeps on going up.

We walked around a lot afterwards, until the dark got too dark, and then we were in her car and I was trapped. She kissed me again. I kissed her back, all the time wondering how to stop it gracefully. She wanted to go all the way and I had no excuse. All I wanted to do was go home to sleep because I had to start work at 6:30 the next morning, and the night before I'd been with *him* 'til very late. So late that the birds were already singing when I got home.

I'm tired of the conversations about being gay and the story of how we met, which she tells me over and over again. I was amused the first time but frankly I'm sick of hearing about how nice and how sexy I am. (And *hot*, don't forget *hot*.) That's all the story she has in her, there's nothing else.

Back to the kissing; again, all hot n' panting but no sensuality. Her hand would slip down my top (down, not up, because I was leaning towards her), and I'd let her touch me a bit before withdrawing and telling her I didn't want to go too far. She wouldn't take no for an answer and would start all over again, offering me her breasts and her body and seriously, I had to say no over n' over again. If she wants to get me addicted to her she needs to press her full body against me, none of this desperate grabby stuff. I need to feel body heat and a different kind of touch. Like his warm hands the night before – she couldn't compete with that. She doesn't know she *is* competing with that. She doesn't know there *is no* competition.

I'm a bad, bad person, and this is surreal. Surely there are more important things to write about than this. These people are sapping the content from my brain and replacing it with pap.

Friday, 21st December, 2012.

Angst free
Now that I've finished at Art Skool, I don't have to be in a hundred places. I don't have to be anywhere else. It's hard to get my head around this; I'm *allowed* to be here. I'm even *meant* to be here. For as long as I want. This place is mine! (Shared, but still.) Funny how I didn't realise that before.

These days I feel my age, although by mid-afternoon I start to feel somebody else's age, and I don't know who that somebody is but I think they're about ninety-two. Maybe it's part of the post-studying collapse?

Tuesday, 25th December, 2012.

Three Little Words
He went n' said them, didn't he. He kept talking about '*this thing that's happening between us*', and then somewhere in the middle of sex he

said '*I love you*' and tried to guilt trip me into going on a proper dinner date with him. Which is against the rules. As are the three little words. The penalty is: I have to call it off.

Dammit. He's been saying it's good that I don't want a relationship because he's not ready for one. He's been saying it A LOT. For me, obviously, because we both know it's not true. But I like that he was willing to pretend for my sake. It showed that he knew what not to expect from me.

In the same breath, however, he tells me constantly that I'm the best thing that's happened to him. And just about every time I finish a sentence he says '*You're wonderful*' and goes all dreamy.

Unfortunately I don't get sick of that. I've been so not-up-myself that all of the attention is bringing me back up to neutral. I'm completely selfish in this case. It's not that I've lost my halo, but I have no idea where I put the thing, so let's call it temporarily misplaced.

I don't want to hurt anybody. But nor do I want to give up such a good sexual rapport. Why oh why did he have to do that?

Monday, 28th December, 2012.

Chaste

Honestly, how stupid is stupid. My most recent lover has said no to more sex, because it's hurting him too much, because he's fallen in love, so it's making him cry.

Him saying no isn't a scenario I'd planned for.

I don't like it, this *no* business. Especially because when I last saw him, in our cubby in our secret place, it was kind of emotional sex. He was raw with the stuff. I was sleepy and this time I didn't mind it. I liked being touched that way. I have mentioned how selfish I am, haven't I?

Him saying no isn't the stupid bit. The stupid bit is that I'm disappointed because I didn't get to have goodbye sex. Once more would do. Like mature adults who know what's what.

Anyway, we'll see what happens. I already know, really. My little prediction? I give him two days.

Saturday, 29th December, 2012.

Somethin's Gotta Give

Writing novel chapters in small snatches of time isn't enough. I need full immersion, and it's getting me down that I'm being pulled in so many directions. All because I don't want to hurt people's feelings. Fuck people. Fuck their feelings. Or don't fuck them, is the point, so that their feelings won't be your problem.

Sage advice.

Have been reading, and with reading comes the fluidity of thought that leads to fluidity with words that leads to voice, which will mean nothing to you but means everything to me because so far I've been writing this novel without a primary emphasis on voice. I usually start with voice, so I feel like I'm doing something wrong without it.

What I have been doing, very useful, is finding the correct balance between story and event, successfully or not I won't know for a while yet. Just, the writing I've been doing is the stuff that happens between the magic, where it's pure hard slog. You know how hard you're working while you're doing it, not painfully aware but aware nonetheless of the non-glamour of it all.

The glamour happens when the voice hits you. Any minute now. I don't know how it's gonna manifest itself; maybe I'll start brushing my hair before I work? Has been a bit of a curly, wild mess for a while, chlorine winning the battle between me and dishevelment. No glamour happening here, only hard work. Not enough of it to make me happy. Not happy, *Jan*. Not yet.

Acknowledgements

Most of the preparation for these volumes has taken place quietly in the shadows – somewhere between Purgatory and Solitary Confinement – where I skulk around as I work. I couldn't survive this lonely business without the feedback of good friends, so thank you to everyone who listened when I leaned out of my turret to scream into the abyss.

Thank you to my mother, for anchoring me in the real world daily, with warm companionship, support,... and an endless supply of chocolate.

A special thank-you to Chris Gabriel for being such an enthusiastic sounding board when I needed to ~~rant~~ think-out-loud, and for your support when I came across inevitable technical problems. Your bystander company was a balm during ad-hoc troubleshooting attempts.

Thank you Tracey Lamb, for friendship and for invaluable practical support.

Thanks also to Sarah Rudledge for being on the technology cheer squad, for generous layout/design advice, and for your practical and moral support. Most of all, though, for teaching me that sharing is the thing that makes "Art" worth it.

Thank you to Diane "Grabby" Glenane, for the sound of your reassuring voice as it echoes across the valley when you call from your own turret. Screaming into the abyss isn't so bad when you know somebody is working away on their own projects at the other end.

Last but not least, thank you to Dr [Empress!] Josephine Browne, for your thoughtful feedback, invaluable conversations, and for *knowing*. Because through all of these endeavours, we are kin xx